RAISE YOUR VOICE

Transforming how you speak,
sing and present

RICHARD LAWTON

FINCH PUBLISHING
SYDNEY

Raise Your Voice

First published in 2017 in Australia and New Zealand by Finch Publishing Pty Limited, ABN 49 057 285 248, 1A, 64 Darley Street, Mona Vale, NSW, 2103, Australia.

17   8 7 6 5 4 3 2 1

Copyright © 2017 Richard Lawton

The author asserts his moral rights in this work throughout the world without waiver. All rights reserved. No part of this publication may be reproduced, stored in a retrieval system or transmitted in any form or by any means (electronic or mechanical, through reprography, digital transmission, recording or otherwise) without the prior written permission of the publisher.

ISBN:9781925048 940

There is a National Library of Australia Cataloguing-in-Publication entry available at the National Library.

Edited by Megan English
Cover and internal typeset by Jo Hunt
Printed by Griffin Press

Reproduction and Communication for educational purposes
The Australian Copyright Act 1968 (the Act) allows a maximum of one chapter or 10% of the pages of this work, whichever is the greater, to be reproduced and/or communicated by any educational institution for its educational purposes provided that the educational institution (or the body that administers it) has given a remuneration notice to Copyright Agency Limited (CAL) under the Act. For details of the CAL licence for educational institutions contact: info@copyright.com.au

The paper used to produce this book is a natural, recyclable product made from wood grown in sustainable plantation forests. The manufacturing processes conform to the environmental regulations in the country of origin.

Finch titles can be viewed and purchased at **www.finch.com.au**

CONTENTS

FOREWORD — vii

PART ONE
1 ALL YOU NEED TO GET STARTED — 1
2 VOICE FOR PRESENTERS — 35
3 BODY LANGUAGE, BODY WISDOM — 71
4 BREATH: OUR CONSTANT COMPANION — 100
5 VOICE AS YOUR GATEWAY TO PERSONAL POWER — 123
6 WOMEN'S VOICE: THE QUIET REVOLUTION — 137

PART TWO
7 SINGING: HOW TO IMPROVE — 155
8 THE LONGING FOR COMMUNITY — 175
9 CHANTING AND MEDITATION — 188
10 VOICE: AN AID TO CURING SOCIETY'S ILLS — 196

PART THREE
11 VOICE AND THE SHADOW — 208
12 VOICE SECRETS FROM THE ACTING PROFESSION — 212

EPILOGUE — 228
RESOURCES — 230
REFERENCES — 231
ACKNOWLEDGEMENTS — 234

For my sisters, and for Mary, without whom this book would not have existed

FOREWORD

What is your relationship with your voice?

Most people don't even realise they have such a relationship until they're asked, which is why I wrote this book – to inspire and encourage people to use their voice to their full capacity.

In over thirty years of countless group and individual singing sessions, I've seen many people trapped in cages. The bars of these cages are the *limitations people place on their voice*, on their personal power and on the energy with which they express themselves, and yet these bars are mostly based on illusion. In fact, most people only use a fraction of their vocal capacity, which limits their personal power and the energy with which they express themselves. Luckily, there is a lot that can be done to take charge of your voice.

When people discover the power of their own voice, it can have far-reaching effects on their life. Their mental and physical wellbeing improves. They feel an increased connection with others. People quit jobs that drain them, negotiate large raises and speak up for the things they care about. And almost universally, people find that unlocking their voice awakens their creativity.

Many people feel they have fragmented, overloaded, discordant lives. One of the reasons for an upsurge of interest in choirs in the last two decades is that in a (good) choir you can experience straightaway the re-integration of breath, body and spirit through voice, and have a great time doing it.

There has also been an upsurge of interest in mindfulness, which utilises attention on the breath. Vocalising and singing quickly put you in touch with your breath and bring you back to the present. When you're reciting good poetry or singing fully, it's actually very hard to in any way multi-task at the same time! Voice can instantly take you to accessing your essential being, beneath all the mind chatter, right now.

This book attempts to pass on some of the secrets, known by actors, singers and presenters, of how to enjoy the power of your voice and how to affect others with this vital instrument. It is divided in three sections to help you find what you need, be that primarily about your singing or your presenting voice. Some chapters are equally relevant to both, especially in Part Three, which carries useful information developed from the craft of acting.

My hope is that this book lights new pathways for all sorts of readers. May it speak to leaders in business and those effecting social change; indeed to anyone who needs to be heard – from presenters, lawyers, teachers and therapists to people who spend a lot of time on the phone and those who want to sing more.

May the stories and lessons contained in *Raise Your Voice* help you to connect with the sound of your voice, and in turn, your authentic self.

ALL YOU NEED TO GET STARTED 1

Do you like the sound of your voice? What effect does your voice have on other people? Which voice is your default setting? Would you like to change your voice in any way?

This chapter will help you answer these questions. I will also share the framework I use in the one-on-one sessions I conduct with clients, which you can use to work by yourself, applying the techniques provided. Also explored are some of the common problems that occur in voice work, including nasality, monotone, the curse of perfectionism and how to project your voice without strain.

Above all, my hope is that this chapter will help you enrich your natural sound.

Your voice speaks to who you are

As mentioned, most people don't realise that they have a relationship with their voice. We speak thousands of words a day yet take it for granted. If our voice were a limb, it would probably be the most powerful one of all. A few words over the phone could drastically affect the life of someone on the other side of the planet.

In fact, we literally speak who we are. The word *persona* comes from the Latin and means 'through sound', which makes a very direct – and unique – link between your character and your voice. Among other things, this explains why voice recognition technology is more reliable than a signature!

Below is a spectrum that captures the different qualities of voice.

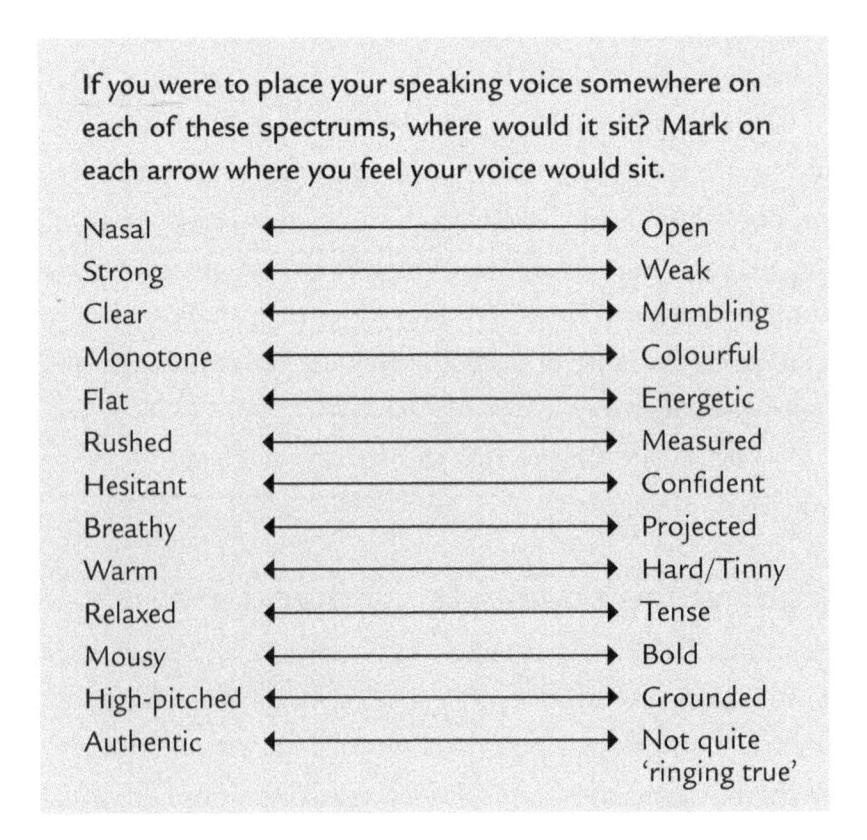

> If you were to place your speaking voice somewhere on each of these spectrums, where would it sit? Mark on each arrow where you feel your voice would sit.
>
> | | | |
> |---|---|---|
> | Nasal | ←——————→ | Open |
> | Strong | ←——————→ | Weak |
> | Clear | ←——————→ | Mumbling |
> | Monotone | ←——————→ | Colourful |
> | Flat | ←——————→ | Energetic |
> | Rushed | ←——————→ | Measured |
> | Hesitant | ←——————→ | Confident |
> | Breathy | ←——————→ | Projected |
> | Warm | ←——————→ | Hard/Tinny |
> | Relaxed | ←——————→ | Tense |
> | Mousy | ←——————→ | Bold |
> | High-pitched | ←——————→ | Grounded |
> | Authentic | ←——————→ | Not quite 'ringing true' |

How did you go with your self-assessment? Many people dislike the sound of their own voice, and yet would be nowhere near as critical of their friends' voices. Test my observation by listening to a couple of friends' voices in your imagination – do you notice yourself feeling affectionate or critical? Most likely it is the former, yet we struggle to apply this to ourselves.

When training groups of people, I've conducted many on-the-spot surveys, and while about 70–80 per cent of the room will have photos of themselves that they like, very few of the same group will say they like hearing their recorded voice.

There's a sad disconnect here – some people spend a fortune on altering their appearance, or on a personal trainer to change their body, yet few people outside the acting profession realise what a profound effect they can have on their persona, and on the people with whom they interact, with even minimal work on their voice.

Our inner critic

Our voice is designed to yell, scream, cry, laugh, hoot, howl and many other sounds besides. We've all heard kids use their full range, but most adults learn to shrink their voice to the size of a suburban living room and then forget where they put it.

If you want an effective voice, a voice that people listen to, a voice that people like to hear, a voice that does you justice, then mere voice exercises alone won't cut it. You'll need to integrate your breath, body and spirit, and that is a lifelong process. We come into this world with these three functions fully integrated, and then life happens. By the time we reach adulthood, we've internalised three characters' voices loud and clear in our head. They are:

- The Judge, who will give you a mark out of ten, usually four or less.
- The Critic, who tells you that not only is what you do junk, but it's the same junk you did last time *and* the time before.
- The Censor, who will tell you to just keep quiet, keep your head down and hopefully it will all go away.

Sound familiar? These voices do have a – albeit minimal – use in our lives. We do need impulse control, and an ability to review our actions. However, when we listen to how the voices in our head speak through these characters, it can be nightmarish. Just lasso one of your own comments and imagine saying it to a friend for some minor mistake – you will see just how out of proportion our internal commentary usually is.

(For a practical tool for dealing with these characters, see the exercise Sword of Truth on page 42.)

Take your time

I have no interest in encouraging you to go chasing an inauthentic voice; one that is not yours. Rather, these pages can help you enrich your natural sound, a sound that expresses a connected head, heart and spirit. That may seem a big ask and we are all works in progress, so this journey needs to start with a healthy dose of self-acceptance. My father used to like the following joke:

> *A tourist driving an expensive convertible pulls into a little village, far from anywhere and realises he's lost. He sees a local in a nearby field and goes over to ask for directions to Wigglesworth. The local says, 'Ooh no, you can't get there from here ...'*

It's a wonderfully absurd reply. I sometimes tell that story in voice sessions, especially if I'm working with a perfectionist. The point is that if you're really hard on yourself and everything you're doing is wrong, you risk not allowing yourself to explore. You'll hold back because somewhere – a long way from here – is how your voice should sound, but it's just too far away.

Indeed, if you start to work on your voice, one of the first hurdles is the impatience you may feel about your voice as it is, and where you think it should be. I encourage people who display these symptoms to be a custodian and carer for their voice. You wouldn't attack someone in your care, rather you would nurture them into some form of improvement – so take time with your own process.

You may say, 'I'm too old to change this now.' But take heart: voice is a very responsive muscle. I've had people in their sixties and seventies come for a session, and even though they've done nothing very energetic with their voice since they were in the school choir, within minutes they notice a significant shift, a freeing up of expressivity.

Framework for an individual voice session

When people come for a session, I usually take them through a process like the one below. You can do this yourself, although it is easier to work with a coach.

Before doing any of these exercises, I encourage you to:

- Commit to the process.
- Set aside time and energy.
- Make sure you're in the right location and not concerned about someone in the next room listening.
- Set a clear intention and time frame for achieving results.
- Have some form of logbook at hand to record the key points.

And finally, a guiding principle for any voice work, which I find myself repeating over and over in sessions, is *easy is right*. If you ever feel any tickling or rasping in the throat, or excessive pressure in the head or sinus cavity, back off, either in pitch or volume. *Easy is right*.

WHERE TO BEGIN

You may wish to record yourself before and after the exercises so you can notice the differences. If you do so, you must be an especially gentle custodian of your voice – most vocal recordings you hear have been heavily worked over by a sound engineer. Moreover, you'll probably be recording on your phone, which will tend to miss out on some of the lower resonances of your voice.

> **TIP:** A simpler, low-tech version for listening to yourself is to cup one hand over your mouth and the other over your ear. You may be pleasantly surprised to discover how much more resonance you can create. (Warning: it may sound LOUD.)

Exercise: Arrive, breathe and connect

1. Stop. Bring your body to stillness, sigh deeply so as to drop beneath the mind's chatter, and connect down into the sensation of the natural rhythm of your breath.
2. Arrive. Sit in a firm chair with your feet on the floor. Close your eyes, take a big sigh, and wait. Connect with a word or image for how you are right now. You may get an answer such as nervous, or buzzing, or relaxed. Write down your answer so that you can compare it with your sensations at the end of your session. It's important to log your progress.
3. Tune into the essential, timeless part of you that exists beneath the mind chatter and current concerns. This is the you that looked out from the same eyes when you were a child. There are much greater forces than us moving around the planet – spirit, soul, divine nature, god, the dharma, the Tao. Whatever you want to call that greater power, you'd be a fool to ignore it, so find a name for it. Tune into it now, and ask for help and guidance to take you into excelling beyond the small, local ego concerns.
4. Ask yourself: what do you like/dislike about your voice? (Answer both.)
5. Ask yourself: what would you like to get out of this session? (Once again, an important step in measuring your progress.)
6. Stand, preferably facing a window so that your voice can 'see' into the distance. (As mentioned, many adults have learned

to shrink their voice to the size of a suburban living room.) Check if there is any tension in your body that could easily be released with a shake or a stretch. (The chapter Body Language, Body Wisdom has more detailed suggestions on this, including the very useful Spinal Roll on page 74.)

7   Stand with your feet slightly wider than your hips, just as you would if you were standing on a train with nothing to hold on to. This should give a strong base, a feeling of being grounded.

8   Take another big sigh, once again tuning in to how the out-breath has a downward sensation, shifting your centre of gravity down lower in the body.

9   Now lift the arms, and as you reach your hands up and forward, blow out as if you are trying to extinguish a distant candle. This sets an intention for your voice to reach beyond the room you are in.

10 Lifting the arms, and hands again, let out a sound, all on one note, to the end of your breath. Work with the intention of sending the sound into the distance. Find a way to connect with that sound, without critique – just let it be. (I know, easier said than done, but try observing the sensation of sound.)

In session, this single note is a diagnostic tool for me. It tells me a lot about the kind of blocks you may have acquired in your past, and where to go next. From here, we progress to working with your specific needs and limitations.

The next stage is usually working with the anatomical obstacles to a free and open sound.

Anatomical obstacles

The neck, mouth and throat can be a bottleneck, constricting the flow of air and sound rushing up from below. The jaw is a particularly crucial body part for those who sound nasal, a resonance that is typified by the Aussie twang.

There are many instances when you might restrict the opening of your mouth. Think of all the times you've had to 'grit your teeth', 'hold your tongue', or 'bite back your anger'. Or you may think it's undignified to open your mouth too wide. The result is that your masseter (chomping) muscle habitually contracts, giving you that lockjaw sound.

By gently massaging the masseter muscle (where your molars are), you can loosen a lockjaw sound. Doing so can also help stop teeth-grinding at night.

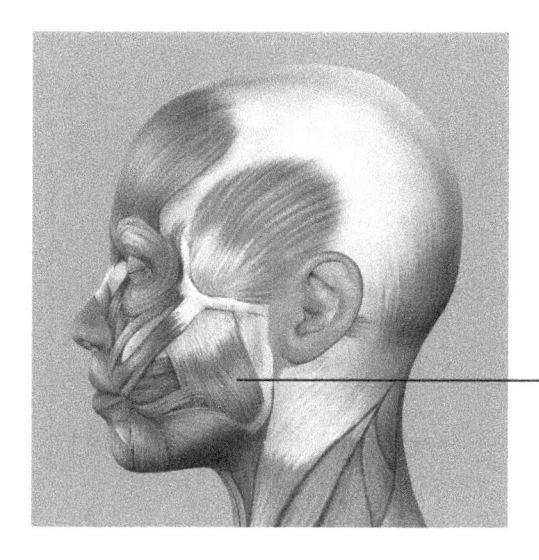

The masseter muscle is a crucial chewing instrument, but can also lead to a constricted voice.

Yawning and stretching are other good antidotes to a tight jaw. This means opening your jaw wide enough for your back teeth to be seen, or at least for you to find out how much opening is possible. Again, massage your molars through your cheek to soften that masseter muscle. Take this slowly. Be patient.

> **TIP:** Focusing on opening the front teeth wide may cause a mild choking sensation, like trying to swallow a grapefruit. This will cause parts of your throat to contract in defence – the opposite of what you need. Most people, when they focus on putting space between the back teeth, generally open the back of the tongue and the lower throat wider, making for a freer passage of sound.

Following are some other exercises to help with nasality.

ANOTHER ANTIDOTE TO NASALITY

If you've often had to hold your tongue, then your tongue might 'hold back'. The tongue is a strong muscle, and the tip of your tongue can actually contract backwards into the base of your tongue. As a result, the base of the tongue swells and fills the back of the mouth. This blocks the exit for air and sound, which must escape somehow, so it will come out through the nose – hence the nasal sound. Try the following.

1. Place a hand on your upper chest and say a strong, definite 'NNNGGEH', tightening the jaw and deliberately exaggerating that nasal sound.
2. Now lose the 'N' prefix and imagine the back of the tongue being soft, loose, even anaesthetised (as if by the dentist). Let it drop, and the jaw go slack. Now say 'GEH' with this dropping sensation and feel the enhanced vibrations under the hand on the upper chest.
3. Announce your name and address, or have a piece of text handy (you will find one in the Resources section of the book) so that you can test this voice and see if you can integrate the sound into speech.
4. You can test to see if nasality is still there by pinching your nostrils closed. There should be very little alteration in the

sound of your words, except for any m's and n's, which of course close the front of the mouth and naturally block the through-flow of air and sound.
5. You can help reverse the contraction at the base of the tongue. Take hold of each side of the tongue with the thumb and forefinger, and gently pull it out in any direction that feels therapeutic; don't let it be painful. A cloth or paper towel can help you get a grip.

Exercise: The cow

1. Drop to a squat. Reach the hands forward so you are on all fours. With shoulders over wrists, a straight, flat back and a relaxed belly, hang free and cow-like.
2. Blow strongly towards the floor as if you wanted to blow it clean, feeling the belly muscles engage.
3. Make strong, definite 'HUH' sounds, feeling the whole torso engage.
4. Make long, strong, definite 'HERRRR' and 'HAHHHH' sounds to the end of the breath.
5. Speak a piece of chosen text slowly, bouncing each word off the floor like you would bounce a ball. Notice all the lower torso muscles, including the groin and anal sphincter, engage. It's now obvious that you're speaking with the whole torso.
6. Enjoy the ease and the low-end power of your voice, which is supported by your lower back.

Exercise: Up against the wall

1. Lean against the wall with knees unlocked and the lower back pressing into the wall. This should be an easy, almost slouching position. In this position you'll be more aware of the function of the lower back muscles. It also indicates whether you're breathing deeply enough.
2. Poke your fingers into your belly either side of the navel, and do your best 'HO HO HO' like Santa.
3. Notice the bounce of the belly and the lower back muscles. This is where the power comes from; it is your engine room. When you want to increase volume, this is where it comes from, not the throat.
4. Speak some chosen text, sending it to a specific point in the room like an object or picture, or for increased projection, to a definite point out of the window. Speak with intent, rather than just spraying out into space.
5. Move away from the wall, take a firm stance and speak the text to the object again.

Exercise: Give it weight

For gravitas, it's good to try your text with heavy, on the spot jogging, or while lifting objects, swinging them over your head, or sweeping the floor.

Why? Because it helps you draw the sound from lower down in your torso, connecting with the lower body. It also flexes your latissimus dorsi and the quadratus lumborum muscles in your back. This flexing action helps anchor the lungs in a similar way to the box on a violin or guitar amplifying the strings.

The Three Throats

There are three main areas of the throat where potential restrictions may occur.

1. The lower throat – for those who want an authentic, deeper tone

A voice constricted in this area will be thin or squeaky, or may sound a bit like Mr Bean.

Above your vocal folds are your 'false' (or vestibular) vocal folds: two pieces of cartilage joined by a hinge. This acts as a second line of defence after your epiglottis to stop food from going into your lungs. In childhood, these are very flexible but like most muscles, if you don't use 'em you lose 'em and as adults, we rarely give these folds a work-out. Unless, of course, we are Tuvan (Mongolian) throat singing or applying the 'screamo' technique of heavy metal.

If your voice is limited to speaking and doesn't get much opportunity to sing, yell, holler or cry, the vocal folds will slowly contract until they are sitting there like a couple of wooden railway sleepers on the free action of your sound.

Exercise: Activating the 'false' (or vestibular) vocal folds

1. Gently hold your thumb and forefinger around the windpipe just above the larynx. Do a silent giggle with breath and a closed mouth – you should feel your windpipe expand downwards and outwards. If you've found the right place, there will be little or no sound when you breathe strongly in and out.
2. Once you've established where the action is, you can take your hand away and access it at will, whenever you want to open the bottom of your throat to create a fuller sound.

> **TIP:** The way to access this retraction easily is to mimic the onset of a yawn. This will give you a voice sounding like the village idiot, with that characteristic sound that escapes when we yawn. It's good practice for those who feel they need a voice that's lower, but don't want to artificially force the voice down.

2. The middle throat (back of the tongue) – for those who feel a choking sensation when they use a loud voice

1   Stick the tongue as far out as possible, as if you are licking food off your chin.
2   Make a 'BLAAAH' sound of disgust. Use a bit of attitude.
3   Run the tongue all the way around the gums including behind the back molars.
4   Mimic the onset of a yawn, this time focusing on allowing the tongue to drop down and forward.

The tongue is a large and powerful muscle, and since many of us have had to frequently 'hold our tongue' over the years, it can take some time to retrain the anatomy. Once again, patience is key.

Stick out your tongue with attitude. This helps dispel the commands to be polite or hold your tongue!

3. The top of the throat – of most concern to those who want confident high notes when they sing or wish to speak with a colourful range

1. Run a finger backwards along the cleft in the roof of the mouth until you feel the bone of the skull turn to soft rubbery muscle. (Stop before you hit the gag reflex. Yes, that is possible!) This is your soft palate or velar port.
2. Gently push up so that you can feel just where it is.
3. Take your finger out and say the word 'car' on an in-breath and you'll get a bit of a cold minty sensation where the soft palate is.
4. Once you've located it, lift it. One way is to imagine you could push your upper back molars apart. Test this by singing the word 'air' as you climb up the scale. If you've really found how to lift the soft palate, you'll be able to smooth out the gear change that happens in the join between head voice and chest voice. Roughly speaking, your 'head' voice is a high, falsetto tone, and your 'chest' voice is your lower stronger sound. (For more specific information, see the chapter Singing: How to Improve on page 155.)

TIP: If you need a bit more lift, try flaring your nostrils and/or trying to get away from a bad smell. This may help.

The soft palate

Like many muscles, the soft palate was flexible when you came into this world but then life and gravity took over and now it may sag. Take heart – this is an easy one to discover, making a drastic difference to your sound. Working the soft palate is particularly good for people who speak in a flat monotone and want more colour.

When I'm helping people to find more colour, less monotone, I may start with an extravagant line of poetry. It's actually difficult to proclaim a juicy line from Shakespeare in a flat voice. If I have students who are feeling bold, I like to feed them some of his wonderful insults:

'Never hung poison on a fouler toad!'

Or:

'Out of my sight! Thou dost infect mine eyes!'

Straightaway, this gives them permission to open up the waveband of expressivity.

Exercise: Sirens

Another exercise that can help open your range is the simulation of a siren.

1. Take the last two letters of the word 'sing'.
2. Gently slide up and down the scale from the bottom of your vocal range to the top and back.

3   Intoning the 'NG' sound like a siren will take the sound up and out through the nose. (This is the sound we wanted to avoid in the 'nasal' section.)

4   Some people (mostly men) find it hard to go up into 'head' or falsetto voice. One way around this is to gently make little puppy whimpering sounds with the mouth closed, feeling the sound high up in the nose. Once a recognisable puppy sound is produced, open the mouth. (Warning: no pushing force or strain here – gently does it.)

Articulation

Let's assume you've removed all the obstacles to a free-flowing sound. Now the point is that you want to turn this into clear, coherent articulated language.

CONSONANTS

Consonants are produced by the lips, the hard and soft palate, and the tongue, which is the main factor that I'll focus on.

There is a whole body of work that focuses in detail on the articulation of very specific groups of vowels and consonants. Unless you have a particular speech difficulty, you probably won't have much need of these until you have the opportunity to work on a classic text from another century (sad, but true).

For those who really want to find out more, I would point you in the direction of the excellent work done by Cicely Berry in her book *Voice and the Actor*, or Kristin Linklater's *Freeing the Natural Voice*. Actors who need this level of detail should really look for a good voice teacher to guide them through the maze.

Some consonants are formed at the back of the mouth ('g', 'k', 'q' and 'x'). In the interests of simplicity I'll focus on the front of the mouth, particularly the tongue tip, which is responsible for so much subtle articulation that constitutes language. Saying the line below:

Trilling the tongue tip takes us to tight articulation

is quite a difficult thing for many people without tripping over. This is partly because English is a lazy language. You can clench your teeth together, purse your lips and still quite adequately communicate through that tiny aperture.

Most other western languages require you to be able to roll your 'r's, in order to make a slight trilling sound. Even just a small amount of attention to sharpening your 'r' will pay off in terms of giving your voice a boost that suggests clarity and authority.

As a warm-up to trying out any text you want to work with, here are a few exercises to enliven the tip of the tongue.

- Make a 'zzzzz' sound alternating with a soft 'jjjjj'. The pressure build-up behind the tongue focuses the action of the tip.
- The trilling 'motor bike' sound on rising and falling pitches is a very good way in.
- Using the phrase 'Lady Di teases' is a good way to test the accuracy of the three consonants 'l', 'd' and 't'. Close your eyes for greater attention to the inner workings of your mouth as you do this. You may notice that forming the 'l' places the tip of the tongue on the alveolar ridge of the gum (where the top front teeth meet the roof of the mouth). If you slowly articulate the 'd' then the 't', you'll notice that for most people 'l' is furthest forward with most pressure, 'd' a fraction farther back with less pressure, and 't' furthest back with least pressure. Try articulating this mindfully through 'Lady Di teases', noticing how much more awake the tip of your tongue is now. Test this with some of the text on this page.

TIP: The one simple thing that you need to remember to keep your voice clear and articulate, is to focus on emphasising the last consonant at the end of your words. Soon it will be second nature, and you'll step into it with ease.

VOWELS

Consonants close the flow of air and sound to differentiate syllables and thus create structured speech. Conversely, the emotion of a word is carried in the vowels.

The simple exercise I recommend is to sing your text to bring out the colour of your vowels, and even to sing your text without consonants, just the vowels, however nonsensical that sounds. For those who feel that their voice is a bit flat or isn't interesting enough, this is a wonderful antidote.

TONGUE TWISTERS

There are many tongue twisters, but a common pitfall is to just rattle them off as fast as you can on some variation of automatic pilot. It's much better to take it slowly and really inhabit each sound. For this my favourite is:

Which wrist watch? A Swiss wrist watch? Or an Irish wrist watch?

It's deceptively simple, but tricky, and definitely requires you to focus and take your time rather than just pattering out, 'Peter Piper picked a peck of pickled peppers ...'

More obstacles and antidotes

There are many speech obstacles that challenge people everyday, even those who do not think they have any speech problems. Below are some of the more common ones.

TALKING TOO FAST

I often work with highly functional people with mighty brains whose mouths can't keep up with their thought processes. They might say something like, 'How do I talk more slowly?'

If they try to focus on speaking more slowly, they will inevitably wind up confused; it's a bit like trying to drive with the brakes on. To them I say: focus on the clarity of the end consonant of each word. This gives the mind a positive focus. It responds much better when it knows what to do, as opposed to following a negative instruction (i.e. 'stop doing that').

I have seen the same technique work in many voice classes for under- and post-grad performing arts students too. In performance, where they need to focus on character and narrative, when they focused on emphasising the end consonant, words such as 'flight' and 'some money' didn't come out as 'fly' or 'summoning', which made the overall delivery clearer and more colourful.

> **TIP:** When speaking to a room full of people, be it a large or small one, use the above acting technique to make sure that people catch every word, as opposed to just the drift of what you're saying. This is particularly useful if you don't have a microphone.

CASE STUDY

I worked with Siobhan, an Irish woman who was the CFO of a large organisation. She had to present monthly motivational updates to her direct reports, but was criticised for mumbling and being boring by her CEO.

Now it has to be said that Siobhan's accent was thick and she did mumble, so I tried first with an Irish poet, WB Yeats, but he didn't quite click. Then we moved on to Shakespeare, which really brought out the music in her voice. In conjunction with the aforementioned antidote to mumbling – putting the end consonant on each word – her speaking improved.

Interestingly, the exercises gave her permission to open her mouth. In her upbringing, Siobhan had been taught that it's unladylike to open your mouth too wide, or indeed make any loud noises. She discovered that the release of tension in her jaw from the yawning work actually made her smile. It was a wonderful relief. These two factors really brought out the colour in her voice and the CEO was pleased at the transformation.

HIGH-PITCHED, SQUEAKY, MOUSY OR CHILDISH VOICE

As with most of these issues, there is no single quick fix. There needs to be a combination of breath work, vocal muscle work, and a bit of a dig into the belief systems that combine with those physical habits. Having said that, the exercises for loosening the jaw and throat mentioned are a good start, as are the 'Ho! Ho! Ho!'s like Santa on page 14.

People often think that in order to project a bigger sound they need to do something with their throat or stick out their chin or some such. In fact, this is totally counter-productive. These actions up top will stiffen the opening from where the sound is released. Go back to your Santa Claus voice and find out how to make it yours. And remember – easy is right. (Take a look at the chapter Breath: Our Constant Companion on page 100 to support this work.)

CASE STUDY

Arthur was an engineer for a large oil company. He came to me because, as he said, sometimes on the phone his voice was mistaken for a woman's, which no doubt was embarrassing in his profession!

As we worked together, he revealed a little about his early home life. His father left when Arthur was three and he was the apple of his mother's eye, so much so that he gave in to her apparent fear of losing him and played the role of her little man. He was quite introverted, getting excellent scores at school by studying hard, and avoiding the company of the rough boys.

With the onset of puberty, most boys' voices break (which means their vocal folds thickened, making them a bit like the thicker bass strings on the piano). Arthur somehow managed to still produce the high notes despite the thickening of his vocal folds. Inevitably this created compensatory tension around the jaw and base of the tongue, but the exercises listed here, especially the Santa Claus voice, helped him free his adult voice.

A HARSH, PUSHING VOICE

Another common issue is the sergeant major sound – sharp, loud and stiff – from someone who pushes their voice out too hard. It's unpleasant to listen to and results from too much air hitting the vocal folds from below, which causes all kinds of tension up in the neck and jaw.

CASE STUDY

Jeff had been an ardent footy fan since childhood. He also loved to sing, but when he joined a choir the bloke next to him was honest enough to take him to one side and say he was pushy and was bringing down the quality of his section.

When we started working together, it was obvious that we had to start with his breathing pattern. His in-breath had an anxious gasp to it, like someone coming up for air from underwater. I got him to lean his lower back into the wall, knees bent, and feel that his in-breath was pushing his kidneys into the wall.

Then we did the Santa Claus 'Ho! Ho! Ho!' with his fingers pressing either side of his navel, and he could see them bounce with every push of 'Ho'. Now that he knew where the push was coming from, he also knew how to contain it, and relax those muscles in tandem with taming the anxious gasping nature of his breathing. It made a huge difference.

Projecting your voice

The answer to the perennial question of how to project your voice starts with those Santa Claus muscles sending strong clear energy up and out. It also depends on the jaw and throat being free. Next step is to look out the window as far into the distance as possible and call out, 'Hello-o-o-o-h!'

When practising your projecting, you might hit all kinds of reactions that tell you that you're too much, or too loud, or express some concern about the neighbours. You may experience a rasping sensation in the throat from pushing the vocal folds hard and holding back physically and/or mentally. I call this 'driving with the brakes on' and the result is, of course, friction!

This is when you need the help of a good voice coach who can spot your blockages (physical or mental), and help you over those hurdles. There are many reasons for experiencing these reactions (we go into the history of this in the chapter Women's Voice: The Quiet Revolution on page 137). However, yelling is your birthright. You came into this world fully equipped for it, you probably did it a lot in the playground, and your voice likes to do it from time to time, so give yourself permission to let go.

> **TIP:** If you want to keep the intensity and clarity in your singing voice while you turn down the volume, pull the sound back into your belly muscles, not your throat. I sometimes get people to find this by acting as if they're pulling in the slide on a trombone to help gain that sensation of reining the volume in by a (gentle) flex of the belly muscles.

Enhancing the expressivity of your voice

The poem *Jabberwocky* by Lewis Carroll is a good place to start when learning to enhance the colour and variety of your voice.

Jabberwocky was written at the height of Victoria's reign over the British Empire, when there was a particular pride in the Queen's English. It was so popular that many of the words – such as jabber, meaning to speak volubly without much sense – found their way into everyday use to become meaningful nonsense, if you can cope with that oxymoron!

A poem such as this gives you permission to make extravagant proclamations without being too attached to a certain way of sounding. You'll find your own voices that come to you – have fun with it. You may just want to stick with the first verse for ease of working with an unfamiliar text. On the next page are some suggestions as to how to deliver *Jabberwocky*:

- slow speed, low pitch
- slow speed, high pitch
- fast speed at any pitch
- slow speed with meaningful pauses
- as narration to a horror movie
- as opera (yes, sing it!)
- as a story to a room full of toddlers
- as a Scottish stand-up comedian
- as a hellfire-and-damnation preacher.

Now it's your turn. The golden rule is to do this standing up, with at least one hand free to gesticulate. Be extravagant, over-the-top, c'mon! It's about waving a vorpal sword around. Let your dominant hand feel the power!

Jabberwocky, by Lewis Carroll

'Twas brillig, and the slithy toves
Did gyre and gimble in the wabe;
All mimsy were the borogoves,
And the mome raths outgrabe.

'Beware the Jabberwock, my son!
The jaws that bite, the claws that catch!
Beware the Jubjub bird and shun
The frumious Bandersnatch!'

ALL YOU NEED TO GET STARTED

He took his vorpal sword in hand:
Long time the manxome foe he sought –
So rested he by the Tumtum tree,
And stood awhile in thought.

And as in uffish thought he stood,
The Jabberwock, with eye of flame,
Came whiffling through the tulgey wood,
And burbled as it came!

One, two! One, two! And through and through
The vorpal blade went snicker-snack!
He left it dead, and with its head
He went galumphing back.

'And hast thou slain the Jabberwock!
Come to my arms, my beamish boy!
Oh frabjous day! Callooh! Callay!'
He chortled in his joy.

'Twas brillig, and the slithy toves
Did gyre and gimble in the wabe;
All mimsy were the borogoves
And the mome raths outgrabe.

(I'm indebted to David Ball's *Theatre Tips and Strategies for Jury Trials* for reminding me of this wonderful piece of nonsense.)

Working with meaning

Think back to the last time you saw someone reading a prepared speech and how dull and stiff it may have been. When I'm working with people on preparing their presentations, I tell them how important it is to move away from the written text and look the audience in the eye. This means having a handle on your text.

Assuming you don't have a photographic memory, the next best way is to connect with the meaning and mean what you say. Simple isn't it? Personalising the text helps.

PERSONALISING THE TEXT

At the Victorian College of the Arts, during the era that I taught there, a big part of the actor's training was 'dropping in'. Here's a simplified version of that technique.

- Go through your text and underline all the key words, the words that carry meaning, which is most of the ones that aren't conjunctions or prepositions. You choose for yourself how deep you want to go into this.
- In a quiet, centred frame of mind, close your eyes and drop each word into your consciousness. Savour each word, see it, hear it, feel it, link all your personal connections and private significance with each of your chosen words. This takes time.

- Repeat your text to yourself, savouring each word aloud. Don't leave a key word till you're satisfied that you have connected to your personal resonances with it.
- Take the text at normal speed, connecting at speed. Notice that it becomes easier to remember what you have to say now that it's so much more than a bunch of words.

WORKING WITH INTENTION

Working with intention is different from working toward an objective. An objective is some point in the future, while an intention is set in the present; sound happens in the present.

If, for instance, I'm working with an intention to project my voice, assuming I've cleared the major blocks out of the way, I aim for my voice to reach a certain point in the distance and my body knows what to do. The waistband muscles that control the diaphragm kick in and power the air and sound out to a distant point. Intention is often the key to having the particular quality we want in that moment.

When we stand still and make clear, strong sounds, we very quickly bump into the beliefs we have that may be putting limits on our power elsewhere in our life. The trick is to quickly lasso those thoughts as they arise – there's usually some rich emotional material to work with that provides the key to working with intention.

IN BRIEF

- Commit to your practise (for example, the same time each day for seven days).
- Set an intention and work with a logbook.
- Stop, breathe, tune in.
- Loosen the jaw and the lower throat.
- Breathe fully and locate the muscles that pump the breath.
- Stand as if on a train and send a sound beyond the window.
- Let the expansive movement of your arms enhance the sound.
- Explore your chosen sound, song or text.
- Play; enjoy it.
- Overcome anatomical obstacles by loosening your jaw and opening up the Three Throats.
- For clarity, focus on the end consonant.
- For meaning and memorising, personalise the text.
- Work with intention: commit to change.

VOICE FOR PRESENTERS 2

I remember, years ago, going to a gig where the punk poet John Cooper Clarke was doing his solo show in a medium-sized venue that was packed to the rafters. He's a skinny little scarecrow with bird's-nest hair, and a fast, driving, thick, Northern English accent. Suddenly he stopped in mid-sentence and said, ''Ere, 'ow come I'm the only person looking this direction?!'

I'm unlikely to forget that moment, because in a few seconds he'd nailed the dilemma of presenting: 'I'm the only one looking this way. I'm probably the only one standing up, and it brings up all kinds of primal fears of being targeted, assessed, and judged. I'm probably on the verge of something shameful.'

This chapter is here to help presenters overcome this feeling, and is divided into three sections:

- The first section one aims to help you overcome some of the fears involved, using body and breath to your advantage to tame the Judge, the Critic and the Censor. It explores creating a Strong Stance, and a secret weapon called the Sword of Truth.

- The next section two outlines a methodology for structuring.
- The last section three features a sequence of useful tools for your delivery, and tips on networking.

Preparing your presentation

We have all had to deal with nerves at some points in our lives. The veteran actor Sir Laurence Olivier famously used to get very nervous before every performance. He was probably a mad perfectionist. Most actors and trainers discover that with practice, the fear recedes to a form of geared-up dynamic tension that, ideally, helps them to excel.

DEALING WITH NERVES

So let's start with the basics; performance anxiety, and what's happening on the biological level when you're in that situation. Your mind tells your body that you're in a fight/flight situation. Your reptilian brain is now running the show and it is only capable of black and white thinking.

Your body then throws lots of adrenalin into your system, chucking in cortisol to help heal wounds, while your heart rate zooms up, your blood pressure escalates and the blood moves out from your vital organs to your muscles. (By now you may have gone very pale.) Your bladder and bowels want to empty to lighten your load before an intense life or death struggle, hence the nervous trips to the bathroom.

In a work setting, these impulses are blocked by our frontal cortex, which tells us to stand still and look relaxed. In this tug of war, that rush of energy has nowhere to go but the mind, so now with thoughts racing wild, and in unhelpful directions, you stand there and attempt to speak normally while a herd of wild horses charge around inside. In its extreme form, this fear can make some people go so blank they can't see or hear what's in front of them. No wonder so many people hate presenting!

> **TIP:** Ignore anyone who comes up with the ridiculous suggestion to imagine the audience naked. This is pointlessly distracting and may even be downright repulsive.

Now here's the good news. Firstly, the worst part of any presentation is usually the last fifteen minutes of waiting beforehand. If possible, try and wait somewhere private.

Second, if you can find a way to harness those raging hormones you'll be operating at your ultimate capacity. Think fighter pilots making decisions at near impossible speed, mothers lifting a car off their child, or people in battle achieving things (for better or worse) that they wouldn't have thought possible. The key is to enter into a new awareness of the forces surging through your system, grounding yourself in your body and your breath.

GROUND YOURSELF

That energy that has nowhere else to go but the brain needs earthing, just as a lightning rod conducts the power back down to ground. Here are three simple steps to ground yourself.

- **Focus**. Bring your energy back down to your centre of gravity. You'll find it a hand's width below the navel in the bowl of the pelvis. This region coincides with your hara (martial arts) and your core (Pilates).
- **Build a Pyramid**. Put one hand on your lower belly to connect your centre of gravity (the apex) with the soles of the feet meeting the ground (the base of the pyramid).
- **Stand like you would on a train when there's nothing to hold onto**. Doing this makes you stand a little wider, as your feet grip the floor and you ground yourself. This pulls the focus from the frantic brain back down to centre and into the here and now.

When we develop this awareness, this mindfulness, about how we inhabit our body in this moment, we can use it to tame performance anxiety. *Presence requires being in the present.*

CASE STUDY

A client of mine, Justine, had her first gig as MC at a weekend conference for women in business. In two sessions we went through some of the techniques outlined in this book and she felt much more equipped to go ahead.

On the first tea break of the first day the keynote speaker, a woman who she'd always looked up to as a role model, came up to her and politely said that Justine really should consider doing some lessons in presentation. Naturally all the symptoms of panic hit — how was she going to get through the whole weekend with such a vote of no confidence?

Then Justine remembered Building the Pyramid. 'It worked! I stood my ground and delivered what I knew I had to.'

That afternoon her role model gave her presentation and according to Justine, 'She was awful! She mumbled, she rambled and went way over her allotted time.'

I tell this story because it's a wonderful lesson in dealing with your inner critic. Now this may be hard for your inner critic to accept, but most audiences don't want you to screw up. They want to trust that you have a firm hand on the situation so they can relax and focus on the transfer of information.

On the other hand, I recently worked with a room full of barristers on the topic of presenting while being bullied by a judge, a disturbingly common event. In the face of potentially crippling comments on their performance, a key ingredient for them to focus on was to learn how to respond, rather than react.

This means being aware of breath control and posture as a way of staying centred and grounded. The good news is that some simple steps in breath release and standing in a centred and grounded stance pay off. It's similar to that old fake it 'til you make it *maxim; ultimately, the outer stance can control the inner.*

BREATHE

If you can harness it, adrenalin is there to help you go beyond your limits. In fact, it may even secretly be why you put your hand up for a presenting gig in the first place!

Bearing the hormonal facts in mind, try reframing your state. Rename it excited, instead of nervous. That doesn't mean you can't still be nervous, but these sensations are not mutually exclusive. You don't need to lie to yourself either. If you acknowledge that you're in a situation that calls on you to excel, you can use the adrenalin to your advantage.

The next instruction under this kind of pressure? It is in fact the simplest. Blow out! Exhaling uses the body's innate wisdom to bring us back to base. It works in the same way as a sigh of relief. If you try one of those right now, you'll notice the shoulders lift on the in-breath and then on the out-breath the belly releases and the shoulders drop, bringing you back down into the body from a hyperactive mind. (More on this topic in the chapter Breath: Our Constant Companion.)

Remember, FEAR + OXYGEN = ENERGY.

In other words, if you consciously work with your breath, the adrenalin becomes a source of energy and a means by which you excel beyond what you already know.

DEAL WITH THE JUDGE, THE CRITIC AND THE CENSOR

We all had these three characters installed at an early age, and they are responsible for the chatter that brings you down, erodes your confidence and makes you question your ability.

The Judge will give you a mark out of ten (usually three or less). The Critic will tell you that not only is this rubbish, but it's the same rubbish you did last time, and the time before. The Censor will tell you to keep your head down, keep quiet and wait till it all goes away.

Can you imagine how much of your energy is sapped when these three squash your creativity and aliveness? You need to have some answers when these three yell in your ear. Try the following exercises to start.

Taming our internal Judge, Critic and Censor.

Exercise: The Sword of Truth

This device cuts through the rubbish. A small percentage of what those three critics tell you has some value in helping you lift your game. The rest is nonsense. Here's an exercise to help tame their bad behaviour. It's a technique that actors use to help them stay in character, but is wonderful for silencing the voices of negativity inside your mind.

Set aside fifteen minutes to do this exercise properly.

- Make a list of three personal or professional triumphs, however large or small. Go on, do it.
- Now sit with your feet on the floor and your eyes closed (essential). Rest your hands on your knees, palms uppermost.
- Into your dominant hand, imagine you could drop one of those triumphs, close your fingers round it, and hold it aloft like a sword.
- Feel the weight and the power of that sword. It's an archetypal feeling. History has installed it in your DNA. This is your power. Use it well!
- Return your 'sword' hand to your knee and repeat that process twice with each of your chosen triumphs.
- Choose one of your recurring self-criticisms. You've often heard it before so it should be easy to find. Imagine you could drop it into your other hand, crumple it up, and make a very definite gesture of throwing it away.

- Repeat the process twice.
- Return to clasping your 'sword' with your hand resting on your knee, and link that sensation to the sensation of smiling, so you know you can enjoy your triumphs.

This exercise can be used while you're waiting to start your presentation, or waiting your turn to speak at a round-table discussion. With your hand in your lap, you can grasp your sword firmly without anyone else noticing. This is your secret weapon. It works by using your body's strength and wisdom to hold your monkey mind steady and focused on what is useful to you, reining it in from running away with negative self-talk.

CASE STUDY

Robert was an executive who was about four tiers down from the CEO in a global organisation. He knew he was valued for his intellect and knowledge, but somehow it would always be someone else's turn for promotion. HR sent him to me for coaching to help him step up his game. HR also mentioned that Robert 'gets too worked up in meetings, sometimes he can take offence and withdraw'. As part of the coaching progamme I showed him Sword of Truth and the following Crown exercise. He found that holding his 'sword' helped him rein in some of his impulsiveness, and helped him to stay centered and much less reactive to stress. It gave him a new sense of identity that was less likely to wobble under pressure and, as he put it, he no longer had to 'prove his worth'.

Exercise: Put a Crown on Your Head

This works sitting or standing and is particularly useful at a round-table discussion when you want to draw attention to yourself as a confident, reliable source of information.

Sitting tall – your Throne Position

This position tells people that you're calm and collected, and therefore worth listening to (even when you're not sure of that yourself).

- Sit with both feet on the floor, spine upright and free from the back of the chair.
- Take a strong breath in that rolls up your spine as if you could inflate it.
- With a slight lengthening of the back of the neck, put a crown on your head.
- Check that the crown isn't heavy, and the back of the neck stays supple. You can look around with ease.
- Continue to breathe down to the belly.
- Bring your hands together in front of you on the table. This is your Throne Position.

Standing tall – your Strong Stance

Get to know this position so that it becomes your default setting. (This holds true for your Throne Position too.)

- Stand with feet slightly more than shoulder width apart. (Refer to Stand on a Train on page 79.)
- Lift the fingers as if they could touch the corners where the wall meets the ceiling.
- As they lift, drop the shoulders as a counter-balance to the rising arms and finger (shoulders low and wide).
- Repeat. This time take a long breath down into the belly as the hands go up.
- Drop the hands and arms but continue standing as if they're still up above shoulder height.
- Put a crown on your head. Walk around, test and inhabit this Strong Stance. Step into it when you need it.

If you're serious about strengthening your body language, it can be useful to track down an image of a queen or king that fits with the imprint you would like to step into.

Some clients have found this difficult, wanting to avoid old-fashioned notions like the current English Queen, or the many tyrant kings. It is, however, an interesting exercise to find an image of someone who reflects this ideal, and the search itself can help you clarify your values and vision.

'BUT ISN'T THAT FAKE?'

As a theatre director I worked with actors to help them find their authentic character. You might object – 'But they're pretending to be someone else!' – and yet good actors will tell you they're trying to find the truth of their character. They inhabit their character, and the way they think, desire and move.

Likewise, you need to find your authentic presenter identity. It's not fake. We all pass through many identities in the course of a day, with shifts of high and low status. One of the attractions of acting is that it gives you permission to step beyond your everyday self. You can use the same techniques to give yourself permission to be bigger or stronger or more extroverted than you normally are.

RESEARCH YOUR AUDIENCE

You need to have some understanding of who your audience is. Do the research. On the day, if it's possible and not too nerve-racking for you, mill around with your audience before you start. Ask them questions about the problems they have, and also what they enjoy about what they do. This will help take the focus off your nerves and give your agitated brain something useful to do. After all, the brain is at its best when it's solving problems.

Now we'll move on to the next section, to help you with preparing your actual presentation.

Structuring your presentation

Any time you stand in front of an audience with a presentation, however large or small and including one-on-one, or over the phone, you're doing it because you want them to change their behaviour in some way. Don't shy away from that. You're not just passing on information. That could be done in an email. Instead, take ownership of the fact that you want the audience to change their behaviour in some way.

So be clear. Exactly what do you want them to do? You should be able to write that down, very simply, in twenty words or less. If you're agonising about the wording, you need to simplify further. Think, what do you want them to change?

For instance you might say, 'I want this team to engage with the new definition of best practice', or 'I want this team to lift their game around handling complaints.' This will help anchor your presentation, even when you feel your nerves unmoor your logic.

ANCHORING YOUR PRESENTATION WITH THE THREE Ws

A handy way of remembering how to anchor your presentation is to keep coming back to the Three Ws:

- Why are you telling your audience this?
- Which facts, examples and stories will you use?
- What do you want your audience to do?

This list may seem like an oversimplification. In fact, that's its function. It's very easy to get lost in the details, especially if this is a topic you know a lot about and you want to pass on as much as possible in your allotted time. The questions help to lift your viewpoint above the details to check where you are on the map.

If you're interested in going a little deeper on this topic, there's an excellent ten-minute YouTube clip by Bernice McCarthy describing what she calls the 4MAT Model, giving a much more detailed approach to presentation structure and to different people's learning styles. It's ideal for facilitators and trainers.

> **TIP:** It's important that you establish your authority early on. Script your credentials so they are brief, relevant and convincing. Let your audience know why they should sit up and take notice of you.

Below is a summary of the key elements of a successful presentation.

THE OPENING

The first time I heard the phrase 'you never get a second chance to make a first impression', I wanted to disprove it. To this day,

I haven't. If you can't reassure the audience in the first couple of minutes that you're somebody worth listening to, their minds will drift to where they'd rather be, and trying to claw back their attention is like weightlifting.

Your voice and your body language are of vital importance in the first minute; these are the elements that win the audience's trust. (For specific instruction on body language, see the chapter Body Language, Body Wisdom.)

THE HOOK

Start with a hook, something provocative or particularly interesting to the audience in front of you. This lets them know from the outset why they need to listen to you. For instance, the phrase above about first impressions was the opening of a presentation by an image consultant. My urge to disagree meant that she had my attention. Then she held up a horrible multi-coloured tie and chopped it in two with a pair of scissors. Now she really had my attention!

Beware though, if your hook is too provocative, the audience might be so busy disagreeing that they won't listen. A good place to start is to work out what the main pains this audience suffers from are. Find the wound, poke a finger in it, and then tell them you've got the ointment. If that sounds brutal to you then downgrade it to a blister, but avoid taking it down to the level of a paper cut.

WHAT DOES THE AUDIENCE WANT?

Right up-front, your audience needs to see and hear that you're going to give them something useful. This means doing the research and shaping your presentation to the audience's needs, not yours. Let them know what topics you'll be covering, when and if there's time for questions, and what time you will finish (if that's not already established).

It's also a good idea to give a heads-up as to any audience participation and direct audience input. Will there be practical exercises? Revision tasks? Group problem-solving sessions? This alerts your listeners to the prospect of active involvement, ensuring that they do not settle in for a morning or afternoon of 'zoning out'. And if needs be, tell them to turn off their phones.

What is your desired effect on your audience?

When I worked as a theatre director, it was obvious that good actors knew that it wasn't all about them. In the same way, your presentation is not about you – it's about having an effect on your audience and getting them to change their behaviour in some way.

When you take the focus off yourself, you're a long way toward reducing nervousness. In acting training, this is known as 'playing your action'. In this case, usually on the other actors in the scene. This was always one my favourite parts of rehearsal. The excitement lies in working together to find the exact right verb that summons up the subtleties of that particular human interaction.

When actors couldn't get clear on what action they were playing, I would get them to 'physicalise' it – the body speaks louder than words. The action is always a verb, and directed at another person, for instance, 'I persuade you ...' or 'I interrogate you ...'

Similarly, when coaching people, I ask them to express what they want to achieve in a simple, physical gesture. There are usually three basic gestures to choose from:

- Uplift – hands start with an 'all rise' gesture. This is optimistic; you want to motivate your audience towards something.
- Prod – finger does a jabbing gesture. You want to warn or alarm your audience away from something and stop them going in a certain direction.
- Soothe – hands spread down and outwards, like a massage. This is calming, reassuring or rewarding.

This technique may seem a bit of an oversimplification at first, but it certainly asks you to be clear about the effect you're having and helps cut out the waffle, which is a huge inhibitor to effective communication.

THREE TAKE-HOME MESSAGES

You may have given us a brilliant presentation, but tomorrow we will forget most of what you said. (I'm sorry, we're human.) So underline your three take-home messages.

(Three is the magic number in the human psyche. We are drawn to the archetype of the holy trinity – three is company, four is a crowd; fairy stories grant the protagonist three wishes; in a joke, the punchline comes third in the sequence; and all stories and drama run off the basic triad of Initiate, Help and Oppose.)

Go beyond the trinity and our memory of your talk will struggle. So no more than three take-home messages.

CALL TO ACTION

This is the basic element of presenting and yet people get so wrapped up in their story that they forget it, ridiculously often. When structuring your presentation, prepare to tell the audience what you want them to do. Put it in the form of challenge: 'How could you apply this in the next twenty-four hours?' 'What is one way that you could apply what you discovered today?'

Without this, I guarantee you people will remember very little of what you said five minutes after they have walked out and started on their emails.

THE 'POST-IT' METHOD OF STRUCTURING

This is something I first learned as a theatre director when devising shows that worked from ideas, not a script. It's a very efficient way of taking a cascade of ideas and marshalling them quickly into order. It's especially handy if you find that you're procrastinating because the task seems too big. The other benefit of this structure is that it's so much easier to remember where you are in your presentation when you know which section you're in.

Simply jot down all your ideas as fast as they come to you. Don't censor yourself. It's easier to free-flow on larger paper or a keyboard first. Just lasso the ideas as fast as you can.

When you feel that stage is complete, transfer them onto the Post-it notes and find a large, smooth surface to stick them on, in any order. (I have a floor-to-ceiling window in my office.)

Next you may find that they start to group themselves quite obviously into the Three Ws. (Sometimes it can be useful to subdivide the middle 'W', which technically makes four sections.)

Don't forget to:

- make sure your opening section has a hook and includes your supporting information as to why the audience needs to hear from you
- include the bulk and the background details of your message
- include ways they can implement the changes you're asking of them (methodologies, resources etc.)
- summarise the main points
- include a conclusion and your Call to Action.

TELL STORIES

The best stories are case studies or anecdotes with a (relevant) punchline. A week after your talk, this is what people will remember most vividly, so hang the information you really want them to remember off something with a plot.

Rehearse the story so it runs smoothly. You may be someone who says, 'I'm not good at telling stories', or 'I don't know where to start.' Don't get stuck there; it's a learnable skill.

> **TIP:** Practise with a friend. Observe yourself describing an incident you know well. A good place to start is with a person, a time, or a place:
>
> - **Person** – 'This guy stepped in front of a bus ...'
> - **Time** – 'Last Christmas, I was just about to start wrapping the presents when ...'
> - **Place** – 'There's a piazza in Venice that has an unusual history ...'

Consider using a flip chart or a whiteboard. This is more dynamic than flicking a remote, and sometimes makes your point stronger.

REHEARSE YOUR OPENING AND CALL TO ACTION

You will need to know these elements off by heart so there's no fumble. Remember, the audience wants to know they can trust you not to waste their time, so test your Opening and Call to Action with a friend. This will help you install it and help take away any stilted, pre-programmed feel.

Having heard yourself perform, you may find that you need to change the tone of your talk, or you may want to recalibrate it from a being lecture to a conversation between you and your listener.

> **TIP:** Find a couple of friends who will sit there while you deliver the whole presentation then give you honest feedback. Your mind may come up with all kinds of reasons not to do this – it feels embarrassing to perform to people you know, you don't want to take up their time, it's probably pretty good as it is … Do it anyway. I guarantee you will find places that show up glaring errors in your script, and it's so much better to find out with friends than on the day with clients.

You should know your material well enough to move away from your notes as much as possible. It can be useful to summarise it into headings, then use your headings like a ladder. As long as you know which rung you're on, you can't get too lost.

I also suggest no more than seven rungs to your ladder. (Seven is another magic number as far as patterns that the brain recognises.) That way, if you do lose track (and even the best people do), you can glance at your ladder and it won't take long to identify where you are.

AND FINALLY, TO RECORD OR NOT TO RECORD?

Opinions vary as to the wisdom of recording your rehearsals. I'm in favour.

Use every bit of preparation you can, with a caveat: you're used to hearing audio that has been recorded with expensive mikes and treated by a sound engineer, which can really flatter the speaker's voice. You will be recording without all these embellishments, so your final product may seem rather rough.

Similarly, if you're filming yourself, bear in mind that you're used to seeing TV and film that's been rehearsed, carefully lit, made-up, edited. It's performed by professionals who know how to look good on camera, and shot with very expensive production values.

One of the first things you'll notice is that your lighting is probably very unflattering, and that you have all kinds of extraneous gestures that actors are trained to eliminate, and lots of 'ums' and 'ahs'.

If you do record yourself (and I recommend you do), then be very generous with yourself. Talk to yourself through the next stage of learning like you would a child you wish to nurture.

Delivering your presentation

When it comes to actually delivering your presentation, there are a few things to remember which will help you engage the audience's attention and deliver an effective talk.

AVOID DEATH BY POWERPOINT

That phrase is a cliché now, but people still commit this sin so I'll be specific. PowerPoint should speak to the part of our brain that responds to visual stimulus. A picture speaks a thousand words, so find memorable pictures and don't cram your slides with lots of text.

If you can't express your message in bullet points, perhaps it shouldn't be there. Detailed or supplementary information can be offered as a handout. You can give the audience a chance to read it beforehand, or invite them to go through it after the session.

Whatever you do, avoid reading lengthy bits of text from your slides. I don't know about you, but I can read pretty fast. You certainly can't speak as fast as I can read and if you do speak, I'm torn between listening to you and reading at my speed. I'll probably do neither of these properly.

Indicate certain significant key points on a slide (headings on a chart for instance), but consider they are there as a visual aid only. They are there to help you, not take up all the attention. An effective slide show brings the audience's attention back to you and your message.

> **TIP:** Try using as few slides as possible. Do NOT use slides as substitute for a script, otherwise you'll be talking to the wall rather than people. See if you can reduce each slide to the essentials.
>
> When a slide has had its value, think about hitting the 'b' key which will black-out the screen. Hit any key to return to the slide. Once again, that takes the audience away from being hypnotised by a screen, and back to you and your message.

MOVING AROUND THE SPACE

If at all possible, check out the space before anyone else arrives. As an ex-theatre director, I wouldn't dream of staging anything without stepping into the space first and looking for where the strong and weak positions are on the stage, and visualising the audience being on the receiving end. Without this you run the risk of being a bunny in the headlights.

I'm in favour of moving around a lot, and *not* getting stuck behind the lectern. That's only a last resort for those who are so nervous they must hang on to the woodwork so they don't fall over!

If you're on the same level as your audience, consider the possibility of coming closer to the front row if you want to create more intimacy as, for instance, when you tell a story or reveal something about yourself. For delivering facts and figures stay further back. I have a colleague who coaches people in the significance of six different areas of the 'stage', but for our purposes all you need to know is when to move forwards or backwards or left or right.

Let your audience see a living, breathing body. After all, that's why you didn't just send the information in an email. You may, for instance, try moving from left to middle to right across the stage when the talk shifts from the past to the future. (Westerners are used to reading from left to right.)

You can get a similar effect when you indicate behind you for the past, and a strong forward gesture toward the future. If you're delivering in a room with a centre aisle or tables, use any opportunity you can to move offstage and get among the crowd. This injects a more exciting dynamic, and people pay more attention when you move closer to them.

FIND YOUR POWER SPOT

Work out where the strongest position is before you start your presentation. It will most likely be central and furthest from the entry, depending on the layout and the furniture.

Before you begin, if there is furniture in the way, ask to have it moved. Work out where the projector image limits are and find a way to mark them, either from the pattern of the carpet or in relation to the furniture. And of course, avoid standing in the light of the projector.

HOLD YOUR AUDIENCE WHERE YOU WANT THEM

An extension of that previously mentioned actor's technique of *'playing your action'*, is to imagine you could wrap your arms around the audience and hold them in place as if you were a carer or tour guide. What is the journey you want to take them on?

This helps take the focus off yourself and your anxieties, and shifts it onto your task with these people. To do this, ideally you need to visit the room before it all starts and lift your arms to practise including everyone in the room. You can practise that at home, and if the room is not available before your presentation, then go to the bathroom and practise raising your arms in a cubicle – yes really! It's good to give your busy mind something useful to do too.

ARRIVE, BREATHE, CONNECT

Taking the time to start on your own terms can help calm the 'bunny in the headlights' feeling. I use a preliminary process that can be memorised as ABC.

- Arrive (A) – at your chosen power spot. In other words, arrive in your body. Feel your feet in your shoes and take your Strong Stance with a clear sense of what action you want to play on the audience.

- Breathe (B) – this is essential to bringing you into the moment and optimising your calmness. Take a breath and exhale slowly.
- Connect (C) – with yourself and remember the importance of grounding. Connect with your intention. Remember to implement your chosen action as a way of affecting your audience and taking the focus off you. That might involve smiling at a safe face (choose three safe faces – near, middle and far), and connecting. The people nearby will feel the connection too.
- The adrenalin you are producing may want you to rush this bit – tame it! That extra three seconds of clock time will really help.

CASE STUDY

I was running a workshop for lawyers in a mid-tier firm, and at one point they asked me to help them with that elusive quality, 'gravitas'. After we'd gone over the significance of the above ABC rule, they each had their turn at standing up front and delivering a short address. Ninety per cent of them muffed their beginning, and metaphorically stumbled into their opening. Practise your opening moment (first impressions, remember!). If it feels scary to take up that two extra seconds then watch Barack Obama's use of the pause in his speeches. Maybe he'll help convince you not to rush.

Build into your talk some places where you can pause. (Make sure you rehearse them properly or you may bale out when you're on the spot.)

This works to emphasise your key points. Think about your take-home messages. Use a pause before and/or after to reinforce them. This takes courage, but hey, it takes courage to stand up there, so why not?

CASE STUDY

I had a free ticket to an expensive talk by an American money guru. Three-hundred people packed into a large room, chomped on the free mints and diligently took notes with the free pens on the free notepads.

At one point, the guru said, 'Write this down. This alone is worth the price of the weekend. [Pause.] It is better to give [pause] than it is [pause] to receive.'

And three-hundred diligent pens scribbled away. I was gobsmacked. These people were actually writing this down! Maybe I was less hypnotised because I hadn't paid to be there, but you get the point — the pause works.

PASSION IS BETTER THAN COMEDY

If you're not naturally a comedian, then don't try too hard to be funny. (Actors choose the character traits that fit and then rehearse them.)

List the character traits you already have that serve your purpose and then rehearse them so that they predominate and supersede those things you didn't like that you saw on playback. (To really do this properly you need an outside eye or coach to guide you through the blind spots. That can make a huge difference.)

Which leads me to an important technique that all actors must learn: know how to play the Status Game. When presenting, it's important to have this one under control. The following information is also especially handy for networking situations.

DON'T SHY AWAY FROM THE STATUS GAME

Animals do it. They always know exactly where they stand in the pecking order. Humans do it, we're usually just not so aware that we're giving off subtle signals that either say, 'This is my patch ...' or 'Don't bite, I'm harmless.'

In conflict, cats and dogs raise their fur and snakes rear up to appear larger. Now, humans don't need such life and death situations or even to be in conflict to be able to make those shifts in body language that help them take command of a room.

> **TIP:** Imagine watching two people in conversation. One of them keeps nodding their head, maybe adding an 'uh-huh' of agreement. The other person keeps their head pretty still. (They probably read the bit about putting a crown on your head.) Your body language radar would tell you that the latter person has the power (professional listeners such as coaches and counsellors excluded). If you're a 'nodder', hold the picture of the person in front of you steady, as you would if you were holding a camera, filming them. Focus especially on keeping their eyes in sharp focus. This should help redress your sense of the power imbalance.

This subject is covered thoroughly in the chapter Body Language, Body Wisdom, but for now here's the quick guide.

There are ways to raise your status, as follows.

1. Hold eye contact a little longer than you're used to – we're not talking out-staring or hypnotising here, just sending a signal that you're focused and listening. Remember, low-status people daren't hold eye contact for long. (For an excellent illustration of this, look up 'Michael Caine does not blink' on YouTube.) This will convey a similar message.

> **TIP:** If you're shy and/or introverted and you find holding eye contact hard to do, then get curious about the other person. Specifically, check and see if you can tell exactly what colour their eyes are. From there it's a short hop to finding out what their eyes are really telling you.

2. Slow your heart rate down – to find out how this works, put one hand on your navel, prolong the in-breath and let it push the hand forward and outward, releasing the out-breath like a mini sigh of relief. Repeat for a minute or more. This one is very handy when you're waiting for your turn to speak, and I defy anyone waiting their turn in a roundtable discussion not to feel their heart rate go up. Knowing how to breathe down into the belly in a high-stress situation brings you back to your wiser self and gives you an inner sense of calm, centred readiness for anything.

3. Take control of your body language – presentation is all about presence; inhabiting this body in the present. So get familiar with your Strong Stance and then, just as an actor learns how their character moves, ask yourself how does Strong Stance sit, stand and walk? Take your Strong Stance into a crowd and play with extending your personal space. Take it onto a train, and now take it into a networking situation and see how that can really serve you.

> **TIP:** Just for fun, when walking down the street, practise your high-status persona and be the one who walks closest to the building side of the street. Try this in or out of rush hour, and every so often you'll come across someone who doesn't want to give way to you. (This is entertaining as long as you're not attached to the outcome!) The next step, which is highly recommended practice for anyone who feels the world is bigger than they are, is to imagine the bows of a ship in front of your centre (around your belly button), and move slowly and purposefully through the crowd. It can be a bit scary at first, but hang in there and you will turbocharge your Strong Stance.

Research from Harvard Business School shows that knowing how to take up a powerful pose raises your testosterone level (the dominance hormone) and lowers your cortisol (the stress hormone). If you know how to stand tall, whatever your height, people will be ready to listen to you.

Psychology has for years named this the halo effect. In fact, research shows that we tend to give more credence to conventionally good-looking people. To this end, while I cannot change people's glamour rating, I can teach them ways to radiate strength and confidence. I've found that when I show people how to put an imaginary crown on their head, they can usually discover a greater sense of self.

CASE STUDY

Devadasi was a petite, female lawyer. She wore glasses, partly because she thought it made her look more intelligent. In her section (mergers and acquisitions), she was one of the few women on her floor, and often had to physically look up to her colleagues.

She was naturally feisty and very ready for an antidote to being overlooked. As well as the Crown technique, I showed how she could look down her nose at someone, when she needed to raise her status, even though they were taller.

It's about getting the right distance in your personal space and then a certain tilt of the head. With the right use of this combination of techniques, I saw her biosphere grow exponentially. She acquired a definite don't-mess-with-me vibe, one that served her well in a predominantly male office.

ASSERTIVE OR AGGRESSIVE?

For women especially, playing the status game raises the issue of being assertive without being accused of aggression. I hear it's almost impossible, so one solution is for women to get over the need to be liked. Tricky one, that!

Recently, when I was training at the Victorian Bar Association's Reader's Course, several women were indignant, believing I had said that for a woman to be successful in a male-dominated profession she needed to behave like a man. My reply was, 'Not so at all, but you do need to understand the language to interact with it.' (More on this in the chapter Women's Voice.)

When you develop your awareness of high- and low-status body language, you strengthen your ability to read people. It also means you have more choice over how you project yourself in any situation.

This doesn't mean that something should be put on. In fact, what really works best is authenticity; letting your true self shine through. Often, a significant part of the retraining is about trust, discovering that the place to start is yourself, right now, and that you have what it takes to come up with the goods.

A WORD ABOUT NETWORKING

If you develop your Strong Stance, your Inner Aristocrat, and establish what helps you play high status, you'll find it really useful for dealing with networking situations.

I believe there actually are some people who look forward to those milling-around sessions with a canapé in one hand and second-grade wine in the other, but they're few and far between. Encourage yourself with the fact that you now have a couple of secret weapons to handle this.

A word of advice: write down an interesting answer to the question, 'What do you do?' By interesting, I mean give them something that helps them ask for more, not just, 'I'm an accountant.'

For instance, I might say, 'I help people find the key to their cage', or 'I help people find their true voice.' Have a couple of brief stories that illustrate what you mean; pithy, with a punchline. Don't leave it to chance, find exactly the right wording that you feel happy about, striking a balance between big-noting yourself and being mousy.

> **TIP:** Eat beforehand. Then you don't have to deal with food and a serviette while trying to hand out your card. Above all, don't eat and drink at the same time. You can't shake hands, and you definitely won't look high-status, just desperate – or greedy!

By now I'm hoping that I've given you enough clues to get to the place where you can really be alive and present during your time out front, and therefore actually enjoy at least some of your presenting. Let's face it, we all want to be seen and heard at least some of the time. Get out there and enjoy the showbiz.

After all, as Friedrich Nietzsche has oft been quoted saying, *'Was mich nicht umbringt, macht mich stärker.'* (What doesn't kill me makes me stronger.)

IN BRIEF

- Deal with your nerves by practising grounding, standing like you're on a train, blowing out and finding your Strong Stance.
- Install your Sword of Truth.
- Put a Crown on Your Head and celebrate your Inner Aristocrat.
- Structure your presentation.
- Remember your Three Ws – Why are you telling them this? Which details do you want to include? What do you want them to do?
- What's the hook?
- What effect do you want to have? Uplift, prod or soothe?
- Remember your Call to Action.
- Remember your ABCs (Arrive, Breathe, Connect).
- Raise your status to take command of the room.

BODY LANGUAGE, BODY WISDOM 3

The soul desires to dwell in the body, for without it, it can neither act nor feel.

Leonardo da Vinci

In this chapter, you will find tips for recognising the body's signals to you and learn how grounding your body's energy and maintaining stillness will enhance your gravitas. You'll see how your body language can influence your state of mind, you'll find tips on eye contact, how to use the Status Game to your advantage in commanding the room, and finally a couple of stress busters.

Why devote a whole chapter on the body in a book about voice? Because using a full voice, in either speaking or singing, is a whole-body experience. Most people think of voice as something that comes from your throat, but a full, strong voice comes from the whole torso, and even engages the thigh muscles.

And if you are a presenter, sometimes your body language can speak louder than your voice.

Knowing your body

I've come across many so-called expert pronouncements on body language. (My favourite to ignore is 'never make symmetrical gestures.') You'll hear all kinds of complicated do's and don'ts that could tie you in knots, and certainly take you away from being yourself. If you use this chapter to find out how to Build a Pyramid, and take up space, you'll have a Strong Stance that is a solid container for your authentic presence.

So many people devote most of their focus to how their body looks in the mirror. This can cause a disconnect between the viewer and the body. In our saner moments, we know that the mirror is not an objective picture of who we are, but merely a reflection of our current mood and focus.

What proportion of that picture is interwoven with some form (however slight) of self-loathing or other negative attitude? As the seminal twentieth-century choreographer Martha Graham said, 'The body does not lie.'

Without our body we would have very few ways of implementing our thoughts and desires. Often we drive it to do what we want, be that at the gym (gotta look thinner/bulkier) or by overcoming the need for rest when we're tired, pushing through when we're sick, or maybe just expecting it to get on with the job of digestion without complaint when we overeat.

Our body will give reliable information about where we are right now in space, in society, and what the current situation really requires from us. It's a guide to living in the present.

So where do we go for the useful information? The answer lies not in looking, but in listening.

How well do you recognise your body's signals?

Stop. Close your eyes, if only for a few seconds. Breathe out, and check in. What signals are you receiving from your body right now? If you're busy or stressed, you may not get an answer right away. Be patient, let the noise subside, and you may notice sensations of anxiety, anger, excitement, sadness, or they may come in less coherent form such as stretched, or confused. This step is very important so don't skip it.

If you want to get somewhere, it helps to know where you're starting from. Consider the following.

- Whether you are sitting or standing, is your spine upright and aligned right now? Or is it in some way slumped or twisted?
- Are your shoulders succumbing to desk-and-screen slump? If so, do you know how to counteract that?
- When sitting, are your hip sockets and pelvis (the foundation of your spine) balanced evenly on your seat?
- Sitting or standing, are your toes relaxed or are they in any way contracted with tension that cuts you off from staying grounded?
- When standing, are your toes turned in or out?

THE SPINE

Learning how to naturally elongate your spine makes you look more impressive and possibly even younger. If you know how to stand tall, whatever your height (Napoleon was pretty short), people will be ready to listen to you.

There is a caveat here. Mere posturing will not get you very far. Your best bet is to work with a coach you trust to bring out your authenticity.

Your spine is central to your nervous and structural systems. Befriend your spine and you will save yourself a lot of pain and bills down the track.

Try doing the following exercise with some music at low volume, something slow and soothing.

Exercise: the Spinal Roll

Here's a very simple body-listening exercise that could save you a fortune in chiropractor's bills.

- Stand tall with feet shoulder-width apart.
- Keeping the shoulders in place, let the eye focus roll down to the floor. Let the crown of the head follow the eyes, and breathe out.
- When the eye focus starts to roll across the floor, let the crown of the head take over as gravity starts to pull it towards the centre of the earth. Unlock the knees and sigh.

- Continue to breathe out with eyes closed. (This may feel a little uncomfortable or disorienting, but persist if you can because the act of closing the eyes and shutting out the world is a form of surrender. This letting go also helps dispel any tension or unconscious holding on that may have been happening in your back.)
- Just hang and breathe out, sighing or groaning if something is aching.
- If you feel like it, pull up on the quadriceps above the knees to straighten and stretch the hamstrings. Give the head a little nod and shake 'Yes' or 'No'.
- When's it's time to stand up, start from the base of the spine (knees unlocked). Imagine the lower vertebrae being pulled upwards, like those of a puppet on a string. Feel the pull of the string shift to the thoracic spine and finally to the head, which comes up last.
- Stand tall.

Many people know this exercise in some form, but often miss listening to the body telling them what it wants, where and how; instead, they go through the motions, driving the body rather than relaxing and tuning in to it. Try taking this exercise slowly. Listen to the subtle signals the spine gives, telling you where it is releasing or tense.

Incidentally, the body likes to be upside down sometimes. This reverses the pull of gravity, helps open up space in the joints and muscles, and eases the flow of blood to the brain. For thousands of years, inversions such as head and shoulder stands have been an integral part of yoga practice, so take your time while you are down there.

Finding gravitas

Years ago I was asked by a partner in a mid-tier law firm to bring gravitas to the team. It made me ponder this word, and try to find a way of manifesting it in practical ways that people could adapt to.

As I did, it struck me that one of the downsides of working at a desk and only operating the brain, the eyes and the fingers, is that we lose touch with most of our body. Our mind is very clever and inventive, but it may also be fickle, abstract and given to wild fantasies and projections that have very little grounding in fact.

By contrast, the body gives reliable, tangible information in the here and now – and is therefore a guide to presence. Gravitas is all about presence, and if you can't be present in your body, your voice will reflect that there's something missing.

GRAVITAS STARTS WITH GROUNDING

We spend most of our waking hours in the company of a commentator. This commentator feeds a constant stream of thoughts through our mind, sometimes yelling, sometimes very repetitive, sometimes stuck in a groove that may be negative and unhelpful.

A common mistake is to believe that this commentator is really our self, when in fact it's just a collection of thoughts whizzing by, some useful and congruent to the present, but very often, just the opposite.

If it's true that we can never really get away from this commentator, it's important that we take care of our relationship with this character, rather than letting it run the show, ordering us this way and that. This is where listening to the body is helpful, especially if you spend a lot of your day sitting down to work – it's a reliable place to go when you want to take a break from the mind-chatter.

The problem with spending eight to twelve hours a day sitting at a desk, mainly operating our eyes and fingers, is that we become very top heavy and out of balance. We're already a pretty unstable structure – tall and narrow with the heaviest part at the top – and when we develop our top-heaviness, we start to lose touch with the very physicality that helps us make wise decisions. We lose touch with the ability to tune into what's really going on, and we risk being at the mercy of the fluctuating whims of our thoughts and desires.

This top-heaviness is accentuated when we make some form of presentation. One of the most confronting things about presenting to a group of people, large or small, is the sensation of feeling very exposed; being the only person standing and looking back at a collection of faces. For some, this can evoke a flashback, a submerged memory of some childhood situation that involved shame or chastisement, so no wonder it feels unpleasant.

When we're faced with such a challenge, the fight/flight hormones kick in. The most obvious of these is adrenalin, which is nature's amphetamine. When your thoughts are running wild but your body is frozen by your frontal lobe's instruction to appear composed, it is easy to lose your focus. One tangible solution is to bring the focus down and ground it in your centre of gravity.

If you are standing upright, the physical centre of your mass is a hand's width below the navel in the bowl of the pelvis. This spot is a source of power and can be visualised as an apex to a solid and grounding pyramid. The soles of the feet firmly meeting the ground form the base of the pyramid, and just below your navel, your 'centre' forms the apex. I call this Building the Pyramid.

Exercise: Find your centre of gravity

The following exercise, Stand on a Train, shows you how you can ground yourself as a counter to performance anxiety. It can also be used as a mindfulness tool, and doesn't take long. A more detailed version follows.

- To begin, simply stand like you would when you're on a train, and there's nothing to hold onto. Make your stance a little wider and grip the floor with your feet. (A simplified version of Building the Pyramid.) This should have the effect of grounding not just your body, but also your runaway mind.

Clients have used this Stand on a Train exercise in challenging presentations and reported back with, 'Wow, this actually works!'

If you have a little more time, try the following Find Your Centre of Gravity exercise. The magic of this more detailed version is that it can change your relationship with the earth's gravity, and enhance the sensation of standing on a planet, which is very easy to overlook!

- To actually feel your centre of gravity physically, stand with closed eyes, feet as wide as your hips, and send your attention down to the lower belly and hip sockets.
- Take a deep sigh.

- Shift your weight over to your left so that your left hip socket is directly over your left ankle, with hardly any weight on your right foot.
- Mindfully slide your weight back over to the right, until there is hardly any weight on the left foot. Tune into the sensation of the right hip socket hovering directly over the right ankle.
- Repeat this process until you recognise the feel of your feet and ankles on the ground and the hip sockets above them.
- Imagine a small ball with weight and colour at the midpoint between your hip sockets. Find the midpoint of the hip sockets by balancing left and right, forward and back, so that the imaginary small ball is balancing directly above the midpoint between your ankles. You are now tuning in to your centre of gravity; the physical centre of your mass if you're standing upright. A plumb line dropped from this centre would drop to the midpoint between your ankles, and point to the centre of the earth.
- Tune into the pull of gravity. Shift your weight a little off centre and feel the fluid pull of the planet within the bowl of the pelvis. This coincides with your hara, your core and your second chakra. Here's where you tune in to a source of wisdom, passed down through the ages.
- Notice that whenever you're standing, your feet and hip sockets are constantly involved in a small dance, a balancing act to keep this unstable, tall, thin structure from falling over.

(Try balancing a match upright and you'll notice what an achievement this is!)
- Imagine, feel, and visualise the lower half of the body standing as a pyramid, with the soles of the feet as the base, and your centre of gravity as the apex – strong and grounded.

CASE STUDY

Alan was a senior associate at a global accounting firm. He was a brilliant technician, in a way that was an asset to the firm, but when he was passed over for promotion a second time, HR put him in touch with me.

When he talked, Alan bobbed up and down on his heels, his hands fidgeted and to make it worse, his eyebrows went up and down like those of a character in an old Groucho Marx movie! He was oblivious of these displacement activities his body made, and as a result, didn't inspire trust and confidence as a first impression. Moreover, his voice reflected his body language in jerky stops and starts, the kind that tend to make the listener subconsciously anxious.

So we started with grounding. Straight away this calmed down his heel and hand movements. We worked with slowing down his breathing, and Put a Crown on his Head (see the exercise on pages 44-45.)

This really helped him build his awareness of what the top half of his body was doing, which in turn calmed down the eyebrows. When I filmed him, he could see the transformation, and was surprised at how easy it had been for him to acquire that elusive quality: gravitas.

Your body as your ally

You can change the way you feel and the way people perceive you by changing your body language. In fact, it is possible to shift your mood or your status right now, without waiting for a holiday or a promotion.

Research from the Harvard Business School undertaken by Professor Amy Cuddy's team (see References) shows that knowing how to take up a powerful pose helps you shift your mood and your status upwards. The research found that consciously adopting a high-status physical posture raises your testosterone level, the go-getting hormone, and lowers your cortisol or stress-relief hormone. In other words, the body is instructing the mind to act a certain way. (For centuries, we've tended to assume the opposite.)

Ever since the Enlightenment when science began to take over from superstition and René Descartes made his famous statement, 'I think therefore I am', we've internalised the notion that logic and rationality are the means to tackle all problems, and that our brain is the source of wisdom, responsible for running the show.

Recent advances in neuroscience show us that we have as many neurotransmitters and neuropeptides in our gut as we do in our brain. So this part of our body 'thinks' about the very physical, day-to-day issues of fighting infection and digestion, as well as having this extra sense, or gut instinct, that we are all familiar with.

Our gut asks us to stop and digest new information, which is a slower, more reliable process than making a snap decision. That instinct is what speaks to us when we are uneasy, but not sure why.

HIGH-STATUS POSTURES

Think of the biggest pose you can take, and you'll probably get some version of Leonardo da Vinci's picture, Vitruvian Man (named after the Roman architect Vitruvius who advanced their understanding of proportion and the Golden Mean).

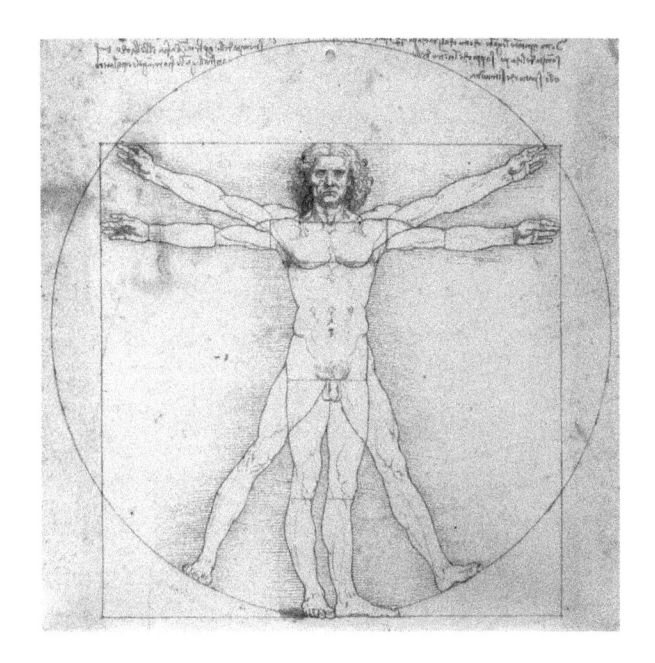

Vitruvian Man

Exercise: Increasing your size

Leonardo da Vinci used this diagram to explain what artists and mathematicians called 'The Golden Mean'. Most people have it imprinted somewhere in their memory, which is why I've used it here to illustrate the following two exercises that will increase your status and sense of power of self.

Explore this exercise for yourself in a place where you can be unobserved and undisturbed.

- Take up the Vitruvian position, making sure that your shoulders are low and wide. Build a Pyramid in the lower half of the body, noticing that your centre is at the midpoint of the 'X' formed by your arms and legs.
- Notice any thoughts that may try to intervene, wanting you to in some way be smaller, e.g. 'This is big-noting myself', or 'This is silly.' Let these thoughts pass through your mind without battling them, observing them with a loose awareness.
- Blow out and drop the arms, giving them a gentle shake in any way that feels like a release of tension.
- Repeat the position with a declaration of the word, 'Yes!' (Why not? It gives the mind something constructive to do and is certainly better than saying 'No'.)
- This time, repeat the position with an image of yourself presenting powerfully and with a clear objective. This helps

take you to a place where you can easily reach out to an audience. One where they can relax because you're telling them you're a person who's warm and confident.

> **TIP:** I do a variation of the Vitruvian exercise whenever I'm about to do an important presentation. If I am unable to be alone, I find a cubicle in a nearby bathroom and do a silent version.

Exercise: Anchoring your gestures

This is another useful exercise, which can be used during a presentation.

- Build a Pyramid by placing one or both hands on the hips, noticing how you're taking up space, presenting a wide front.
- Try this with one hand on the hip and one hand free to indicate with gestures. (This is also a form of grounding – the hand-to-hip connection helps to still any nervous displacement activity, and works by connecting the top half of the body with the pyramid below.)
- Now test this by speaking, using the free hand to emphasise and indicate with gestures.

This woman is anchored, connected, and her body language conveys warmth and confidence.

> **TIP:** In workshops, women have often reacted unfavourably to this pose, saying something like, 'I feel like I'm about to pick a fight with someone', or, 'It's as if I'm about to yell at my kids.' Interestingly, men tend to be more comfortable with this stance.

Body language and the Status Game

Status is present in any human interaction. It's invisible, unspoken, and constantly fluctuating. Status transactions are happening all the time as people unconsciously manoeuvre their way around the situation in order to get what they want.

It's often an elephant in the room, especially in a society such as Australia that likes to lay claim to its classlessness. But whether we bury the thought or not, we usually have a pretty fair idea of where we stand in the pecking order at any one time.

Flexibility of status is one of the keys to self-confidence. If we can shift our position relatively easily up and down the status ladder, we're more able to accept the myriad of consequences of a particular situation – good or bad.

Status is not fixed. It's a transaction of attitude, and how others assess you. For instance, Hitler was a relatively small man with slightly effeminate gestures and a Charlie Chaplin moustache, yet millions worshipped him as a warrior saviour.

Likewise, a homeless person sitting on the ground, eyes down is pretty low status in relation to the executive who walks by. However, the same homeless person with a mad glint in their eye launching at that same executive with a belligerent question probably reverses that status transaction instantly.

Elaine Paton, CEO and author of *Talking Brief*, eloquently describes this connection between flexibility and confidence.

> '*A key element of self-confidence is, therefore, an acceptance of the multiple possible outcomes of any given moment. When one does not dwell on negative consequences one can be more self-confident because one is worrying less about failure or ... the disapproval of others following potential failure. If there is any self-belief component to self-confidence, it is simply a belief in one's ability to tolerate whatever outcome may arise; a certainty that one will cope.*

There are some consistent features that people demonstrating low and high status display. Low status is generally characterised by:

- Avoiding or breaking eye contact
- Gestures that cover up vulnerable parts of the body
- Speaking high and quickly
- Overusing the word 'sorry'
- Keeping physically small
- Being overly mobile and erratic.

While high status is conveyed by:

- Holding eye contact
- Using expansive gestures
- Speaking low and loud
- Assuming or taking up space
- Keeping the head still and the eyes single-focused
- Keeping still until it's time to move.

Try the Put a Crown on Your Head exercise on pages 44–45 to increase your status. This works sitting or standing and is particularly useful when at a round-table discussion and you want to draw attention to yourself as a confident, reliable source.

CASE STUDY

At times in training sessions, people have suggested that Australia is a relatively classless society. As an answer I have been known to do a role-play based on the gender divide. After a bit of discussion and allocating status on a scale of one to ten, I get all the men in the room to walk around in high status (say, an 'eight'). The women meanwhile play a low 'three' or 'four'. They're given a scenario wherein they each have an objective to complete while maintaining this status. I then get them to swap roles. In each version a lot of heat is generated. Afterwards I ask them if the feelings they experienced were familiar, and inevitably most people relate to feeling like the underdog or how good it feels to score a point over someone, and yes, they would like to have a corner office, thank you …

CHARISMA

The good news is that charisma can be trained. And no, you're not a fake if you're taking conscious control of your body language. Just as mindfulness trains us to focus inward on the subtle, physical sensations that bring us into being present, charisma training tunes into those sensations with an outward focus, to send out signals that increase our presence.

By learning the following techniques, you can increase your physical awareness and charisma, and become comfortable in your own skin.

Commanding the room

Some people have a reaction to this phrase, especially in a society as democratic as Australia that has traditionally distrusted tall poppies. But if any part of you shies away from this notion, best capture those thoughts before they scuttle away to hide in your subconscious mind, waiting to sabotage you next time you stand up and speak – they are exactly the thoughts you need to bring front and centre. (For more detail, see the chapter Voice for Presenters.)

It's important to feel comfortable taking up space. This doesn't mean being overly loud or domineering. It means, for instance, when you make hand gestures, having space between your elbows and your torso. It means not being afraid to raise your hands above shoulder height when that's appropriate to your message, and of course, speaking in a voice that unashamedly reaches out to touch everyone in the room. You may be comfortable putting one or both hands on your hip, or when you make gestures they are large and expansive.

Regardless, if you know how to take up space, whatever your gender, then you're on track for taking command of the room.

Eye contact

Low-status physicality is conveyed by avoiding eye contact. So is introversion, which is not to be confused with shyness, or people with an auditory preference, who sometimes watch with their ears.

If you want to enhance your aura of command then maintain strong eye contact. If that's tricky for you then practise in private, expressing your opinions to a fixed point or even in the mirror. (Remember to be kind to yourself in response to that image.)

CASE STUDY

I was invited by the Asian Australian Lawyers Association (AALA) to help some of their members increase their confidence. The association's website talks about the need for Asian lawyers to raise their profile as even though a large percentage of law graduates are Asian, they find themselves seriously under-represented in the higher echelons of the profession.

And while the numbers for female lawyers in the legal profession are poor — in law firms anything over 25 per cent female partnership is regarded as rare and progressive — the numbers for Asian lawyers are worse. They currently represent only 3 per cent of partners, 1.6 per cent of barristers and 0.8 per cent of the judiciary. The AALA speculates that this stems from the fact that Asian people tend to have 'too much respect for authority'.

One of the board members, a lawyer whose parents are Vietnamese, said a phrase she remembered from her childhood was, 'The loudest duck gets shot.' I discovered that the Japanese equivalent is, 'The nail that pops up gets hammered down.'

When it came time to work together on body language, there were many cases of people speaking with their elbows seemingly glued to their ribs. Whenever they felt they'd said something slightly incorrect, a hand went up to the mouth in that international gesture of shame, simultaneously trying to take back the words while hiding the lower face.

Conversely, I've also worked with (mostly male) barristers who were brought up with the sense of entitlement that the 'right' school can instil. Some were very comfortable holding court, even when they had nothing particularly valuable to say. Their stance would often include a slight lift of the chin, one or both hands on hips, and a tone of voice that said, 'Write this down, I'm offering you pearls.'

Grounded stance

How aware are you of your body when under pressure though? Most people don't really notice because their mind is making too much noise, but it's particularly important to ground yourself. Try the exercises Build a Pyramid (page 78) or Stand on the Train (page 79) to give yourself a powerful stance.

Finding a grounded stance: ready for anything.

Contrast this with the picture of the well-dressed executive woman below.

Notice that in the standing position, the upright line is broken into tilting away from strength and confidence, while any tilt of head or shoulders says, 'I'm harmless.'

For women, something to watch out for is standing with ankles crossed – fine if you're hanging out in the coffee queue, but when it's an important presentation or networking situation, it sends an unconscious signal, 'I'm not grounded and solid.'

Although men don't have the added disadvantage of stilettos, they may still have the default setting of being cut off or locked at the knees, and therefore send out subtle signals that say, 'If you push me, I might fall over.'

Destined to wobble: this woman's pose puts her off balance and undermines her power.

Our neck is the part of the spine that is the most common indicator of mental tension. Our shoulders pick up the message and join in. It has been said that the reason our shoulders lift in life-threatening situations is to protect our jugular and the other vulnerable parts of the throat. Whatever the reason, they creep up slowly and imperceptibly when we're under stress.

> **TIP:** Try this as a means of tuning into reversing that process. Imagine a stressful day (don't try too hard!) and, as if in a piece of time-lapse video, slowly creep the shoulders up a few millimetres.
>
> You just gave yourself the fast-forward sensation of your body's response to stress.

Here's a sixty-second stress-buster, which will shift you over to the pleasure side of the spectrum.

Exercise: neck extension

- Reach your right arm over your head and hook your fingertips under your left earlobe. Let both shoulders drop as you blow out.
- Relax into the posture as much as possible for five long out-breaths.

- Bring the arm back down and feel the difference between the left and right sides of your neck.
- Repeat on the other side.

After the first part of the exercise, you may have felt one-sided. It's an instant demonstration of the tension you were holding in your neck, particularly the sternocleidomastoid muscle that goes from your ear to your clavicle.

Driving in rush hour or typing under deadlines brings on this contraction. Before long you're locked into unconsciously operating in a form of low-level fear reaction. This entails holding on to a state of anxiety, and that sixty-second exercise may have just told you what it's like to take some of that load off.

Here is another instant stress-buster.

Exercise: Sighing

- Take a big breath in and sigh (with or without sound).
- Notice your shoulders drop.
- Wait a few seconds until your body is ready to sigh again.
- Repeat three times.

Notice what this does to your mood. Your body, in it's wisdom, is getting you to alter your breathing, drop your shoulders and come back down to your centre.

Recently, I read a wellness advisor writing in *New Lawyer* magazine about screen apnea. She pointed out that when we spend a long time slumped forward over a screen, desktop or phone, we squash down our lungs, creating breathing problems.

What the wellness expert didn't mention is that this posture – chest caved in, shoulders forward – is also the posture of grief. If you followed up the research on body posture mentioned above, you'll realise the danger of long-term drooping into this position. It will inevitably make you depressed.

Our posture greatly affects our mood.

Stand up for yourself and take a deep breath. It may be a valuable antidote to depression.

CASE STUDY

In another century when I started theatre school, my intention was to study acting. When I was told that we had 90 minutes of dance at the beginning of every morning I thought, 'Sure, let's keep fit. Why not?'

Little did I realise that we were in for something much more fascinating and more useful as a code for inhabiting a human body than mere high kicks. To my surprise, we spent a lot of our first term lying on our backs tuning into our breath and anatomy, and then, while standing, we did hours of spinal rolls.

It took me a while to work out why we were studying this instead of hot dance moves, but now I'm eternally grateful to Mary Fulkerson, the wonderful dance teacher who helped us realign our bodies and took us on the journey of a technique called Release.

It was very confronting because we seemed to spend an inordinate amount of time lying on our backs, focusing on breath and different parts of our skeleton. We also spent a lot of time moving with our eyes closed, focusing on the inner workings of our anatomy. My posture started to alter drastically.

Later that year we worked intensively with Steve Paxton, master dancer and the originator of a form called Contact Improvisation. This focused our inner awareness and connected it up with other bodies in a wonderfully acrobatic rolling and lifting free-fall dance. There are Contact Impro classes and jams all over the world, and if you find one it may surprise you, and help you discover what your body is capable of.

Decades later my spine is strong and flexible and rarely gives me any aches despite a damaging bout of Scheuermann's disease in my teens and subsequent falls from a cliff and from a balcony, which did some permanent damage and realignment to my lumbar and thoracic sections. Despite those falls, having these techniques installed in my body's knowing saved me from much worse damage.

I mention this not just to show off (well, maybe a tiny bit) but to make the point that it's important to have some regular form of body movement practice. A lot of us tend to live and work in a sitting-down culture, leaning forwards towards a screen. It's important to befriend the body before middle age if possible and find some sport or dance or other activity that brings you joy.

If it's something that feels too much like hard work, or something you feel you should do because it's good for you, it will slide away into the land of dead New Year's resolutions. Rather, it must be something you look forward to, something that makes you breathe deeply and fully. It must bring you truly alive.

In the words of Walt Whitman, 'I sing the body electric' and 'Not an inch nor a particle of an inch is vile'.

IN BRIEF

- Gravitas starts with grounding.
- Find your centre of gravity.
- Use high-status postures.
- Put a Crown on Your Head – sit and stand tall.
- Use eye contact.
- Befriend your spine with the Spinal Roll.
- Try the stress busters and avoid screen apnea.

4 BREATH: OUR CONSTANT COMPANION

Conscious control of the breath can reduce performance anxiety and bestow many health and wellness benefits. This chapter deals with tuning in to your breath as a source of energy, and as a way of identifying and changing your mood or state of mind. There are instructions for getting the most out of each breath, and we will look at the four basic emotions in the context of breath, and how to use your breath as a stress-release mechanism. Finally, there will be a simple introduction to the use of breath in the practice of mindfulness.

Introduction to breath

Breath. It's always there, wherever we go, whatever we do. Yet we hardly notice this vital function because we tend not to notice what's always there. Still, all day and all night, we ride on this inflating and deflating wave – the most consistent point where our physical being interfaces with the world around it.

> **TIP:** Breath can shift your mood in just a few seconds. Close your eyes and imagine inhaling the fragrance of your favourite flower, perhaps the arrival of the first blossoms of spring. Take a few seconds to linger there, with the fragrance at the forefront of your mind. Pause and ask yourself, did that change your physical or emotional state in any way?

Our breath is the essential ingredient in mindfulness, as well as in speaking, singing and as a means of getting something off your chest. When beginning to work with breath, consider:

- How often do you notice your breath?
- Would you ever consider yourself as someone who doesn't have a lot of breath in reserve?
- Do you think you could slow down your heart rate and lessen anxiety by changing your breath?
- If you take a big deep breath in, what moves most – your belly or your chest and shoulders?

When you see a baby cry, lying on its back, that big Buddha belly is going up and down with each breath. Nature is operating at its most efficient to pump a lot of sound and emotion out of this tiny body.

> Interestingly, Gautama the Buddha was not fat. He was a prince of the noble warrior class, who had by contemporary accounts a beautiful strong body. When he left the palace to become a wandering monk he fasted a lot in his quest to transcend samsara, or the illusions of this world. In China and Japan, devoted meditators wanted to illustrate breathing down to the belly as a meditation practice, and so images of the Buddha grew fat. In India, some images of Gautama depict him as strong and slender.

But as we get older, the price of growing up is, as Shakespeare noted, 'the thousand natural shocks that flesh is heir to'. It becomes rare that we get the opportunity or inclination to lie on our back like a baby and yell or throw any kind of tantrum.

In consequence, we hold back, tense up, and our breathing gets shallower, because that means we'll feel less – less of the hurt or shame that may resurface from our past experiences.

What prevents us from breathing properly?

When you breathe in, can you feel your lower back expand? When you breathe in, does your torso expand upwards or downwards?

There is a huge pressure in western culture to be trim, taut and terrific, but as the waistband muscles squeeze in, we lock off the bottom end of our lung capacity with shallow breaths into the top of the lungs. Now the breath is operating upside-down from the way we knew when we came into the world. In other words, we are breathing into the rib cage rather than the belly.

The trouble with this is that of the twelve ribs we have each side, the top ten are relatively fixed. (The bottom two are not attached to the sternum so they can truly expand on the in-breath.) Now we're trying to breathe and fill up an enclosed cavity (literally, the rib *cage*).

If the breath can't go down or outwards it has to go up, so each in-breath minimally lifts our shoulders, mimicking and repeating a micro reaction to shock or anxiety, which in turn leads to rehearsing a constant, low-level tension that eventually becomes normal.

This problem is magnified under larger stresses such as making a presentation to a room full of people, but if we begin with an increased awareness of exactly what's happening in the body, we can do something about controlling our responses.

How often do you really breathe to your maximum, for instance swimming, running, cycling, dancing? For me it's important to find out, at least once a week, how I breathe at my limit.

CASE STUDY

When I met Robert, he was a man in his forties and a technician, a details person. He was tall with a large frame, but was seriously shy about handling social situations. He had been an avid Aussie Rules player when younger, and talked half-jokingly about the punishment he'd given his body and the regime he'd used to toughen himself to deal with the collisions on the field.

His laugh, when it came, started as a shudder then came out as a harsh, barking sound. At first he found it quite difficult to shift from breathing high in his chest, his stomach locked. But as he slowly breathed deeper, his emotions began to unfold, starting with tears.

Imagine what a huge transgression that would be for a footy player! In time, Robert developed a wonderful rich tenor voice, and now sings wholeheartedly in a choir.

Exercise and breathing properly

Swimming, running and many other types of cardiovascular exercise have the potential to bring strong, releasing breathing. This brings relief because it discharges tension that, combined with the accompanying endorphin rush, may bring you back to feeling comfortable in your own skin.

I wouldn't include weight training in this, because this is an activity designed to create structured tension in the body; namely muscles that look good. I'll admit my bias in that I regard this as a fairly narcissistic activity, which stiffens the body armour. While that may be good for strengthening the bones, it seems to be largely about outer appearance, rather than inner awareness.

In men (and women), it often seems to come from the urge to move through the world like a tank, personified as the comic book superhero whose hard exterior repels bricks and bullets. To me this seems very limited when compared with other movement disciplines, such as dance or martial arts, which coordinate mind and body into moving through the world with harmonious flow and presence.

My brief experience of working a weight-training programme left me feeling sweaty but brain dead, dulling the mind/body connection – pretty much the same as my teenage memories of factory work. It also saddened me to see people on the treadmill (factory work again) watching a row of TV screens while exercising – a classic mind and body split, as if there's a tiresome necessity to move the body, but real life is somewhere else. This is a direct antithesis to mindfulness!

Instructions for breathing

That may sound odd. After all, we came into this world pre-programmed, already knowing how to breathe efficiently. But then life got in the way.

Try the following to bring back your natural breath. Think of it as like pouring water into a glass – it fills from the bottom up. Try doing the same with the air in your lungs, and fill the bottom of your lungs first. It may take some conscious effort at first, and often I have to help people in sessions, so go easy on yourself until you get the hang of it.

STEP 1
- Put your hands on your hips, then a little higher so your thumb and forefinger rest on your bottom rib. Place the thumb quite close in to the spine, level with the kidneys.
- Make sure that your shoulders are low and wide, not tense or lifted.
- Take a long breath in – you should feel the lower ribs expand significantly.
- If you don't feel your thumbs being pushed out and aside, you're probably only breathing the top half of your lungs.

Filling from the bottom up

STEP 2

Take some time out to try the following exercise. On an anatomical level, this exercise encourages a letting go of the psoas muscle (the long, powerful muscle that runs from the top of the thigh bone, through the pelvic bowl to the lower back, connecting the legs to the spine). The psoas influences everything from lower back pain and anxiety, to gut feelings, full body orgasms and pure pleasure. If we are constantly driven forward by deadlines, it will constrict and function inefficiently. We'll be off balance, trying to live in the future. But when it releases, we can have a wonderful appreciation of balancing comfortably in the present moment.

- Lie flat on your back, knees up, soles of the feet on the floor.
- Place about a centimetre of folded towel under the head for padding and a gentle lengthening of the back of the neck.
- Find a position for the feet where the knees can comfortably fall together, letting the weight of the thighs fall into the hip socket. (You could fall asleep and they would stay in place.)
- Place one hand on the belly and feel the rise and fall of the breath.
- Place the other hand on the chest, and check that there's very little lift there; breath happens mostly in the belly.
- Let the in-breath roll down the spine, like a gentle rolling pin, expanding the lower ribs and gently stretching the spine a little longer.

- In doing this, allow the possibility of a wonderful sensation of letting go of responsibilities, of doing, of having to and should.

> **TIP:** If the hand on the belly is barely moving but the chest is rising and falling, it probably means you're only breathing into the top of your lungs and locking off the lower half of the torso. (Sadly, I see this all too often in individual sessions.) This habit might be the result of years of the trim, taut and terrific syndrome, and/or the result of some shock early in life that created a desire to cut off from the belly and its attendant feelings.

CASE STUDY

Delilah was a department head in a mid-size firm. She was a woman in her late forties who came to me to improve her corporate presentation skills. She had been a model till the age of twenty-five, then gave it up and set about getting an education and a different career.

Early on in our working together, Delilah told me that her husband was a cosmetic surgeon and proudly listed the results he'd achieved with her. (She then gave me some fairly detailed instructions as to what he could do for me.)

Even though she was showing signs of menopausal waist thickening, Delilah certainly looked good for her age. Still, I felt there was something brittle and brassy about her image, and in her breathing; she never did let go of her need to be trim, taught and terrific. It seemed as if it would have been terrifying for her to let go. Perhaps her conditioning as a model told her that survival depended on looking forever young.

Remedies

A long-established habit may not shift overnight, but the first step to rebalancing is gaining an awareness of what is. Ideally, this is the snowball that creates the avalanche of change.

The two exercises below help increase the awareness of how the belly muscles drive the voice. People often make the mistake of thinking that to project their voice they must do something with the throat, and accompany that with sticking out the chin. This is totally counter-productive. The power and richness in your voice comes from the belly muscles.

Exercise: Panting

- Press your fingers into your belly either side of the navel.
- Pant like a dog, or blow out an imaginary birthday cake candle, in a way that really moves your fingers.
- This should be a big movement – if not, let yourself go 'fat' and try again.

Exercise: Up against the wall

- Lean against a wall with feet apart and knees unlocked about 20cm away from the wall. This should accentuate the sensation of the lower back being breathed, that is, pushed into the wall by the in-breath.
- There should be almost no movement of the shoulders, especially not upwards.
- Work with the image of pouring water into a balloon, feeling the lower half of the torso fill up and expand down and outwards. There should be an enhanced sense of breathing into the lower back and floating ribs.
- Try the same thing standing free of the wall.

Following is a wgreat exercise I discovered at theatre school.

Exercise: Letting yourself be breathed

- Settle into a constructive rest position, lying on your back, soles of the feet on the floor, knees falling in together.
- With each out-breath allow a sense of relief to seep in, like when you sigh with relief.
- At the end of an out-breath, lie still and wait until the next breath comes in of its own accord. This may take longer and longer as you relax into it.

> **TIP:** This one has been known to stir up mild feelings of panic as a sense of loss of control seeps in, but relax, let go, and it becomes obvious that the notion of commanding your decision to breathe is 99 per cent illusion. As you read these lines you are being breathed. Beyond the panic, there is the possibility of being enormously comforted by how well your body takes care of you. The mind thinks it's running the show, and yet ...

I use the following exercise in presentation seminars to help people know what to do when anxiety or panic strikes.

Exercise: Relieving stress by coming back down to ground

- Take yourself back to the last time you had a nasty (but relatively minor) shock, for instance a near-miss while driving. Be careful not to sink too deeply into the memory!
- Re-enact the adrenalin and cortisol injection your body gave you by conjuring the sensation of panic somewhere in your body. (Most commonly, this occurs in or near your solar plexus.)
- Allow this to trigger a sharp intake of breath.
- Simultaneously lift your shoulders a couple of millimetres to protect the sides (the vulnerable parts) of your neck from attack.

- Stiffen your core muscles and lock your shoulders up tight to brace yourself against the inevitable catastrophe. Of course, it's not going to happen so blow out.
- Feel the shoulders drop and the belly release.
- If standing, then simultaneously include the Building the Pyramid gesture outlined in the previous chapter.

This is a fairly extreme version of what can happen on a micro level several times during a stressful day. That unpleasant encounter, or a few seconds of panic about temporarily losing your phone or wallet, can trigger this bodily reaction.

Without the conscious motion of blowing out and away, that tension doesn't entirely leave your body after the danger has passed, and without some form of release like massage or conscious use of the breath, it may become a chronic, self-perpetuating loop.

> **TIP:** Test your body's wisdom with a sigh of relief. An extended version of this is to blow out strongly through pursed lips, as if you were blowing up a balloon with a 'FFFFFF' sound, which sounds like air escaping from a burst tyre.
>
> Making this strong fricative sound accentuates the unwanted pressure build-up in the belly, in order to release it.

Breath and your mental and emotional state

Most people rarely notice the intricate connection between their breath and their mood. But when we develop this awareness, we can use it to help shift persistent emotions that block us from being available to the present moment.

In my work as a theatre director and teacher, I would often get asked, 'How do I consistently reproduce an emotion?' So I showed the students and actors a model that operates from the premise that while there are many categories of feelings, the four most basic human emotions are fear, pain, anger and love. There are many other models (I particularly like the Hindu model, which includes courage), but the advantage of this one is its simplicity.

Any emotion you may list belongs in one of these categories or is a cocktail of any number of them. When I put the theory to the class and asked for examples of emotions, my favourite was jealousy, because that combines all four!

Let's look at the breathing patterns that match each of these. Try them out for yourself as you sit (or preferably stand), reading this page. If you really want to experience this, take your time, with no distractions, eyes closed, alert to any visual images that may come up.

- Fear – short shallow breaths that only reach the top part of the lungs, shoulders lifted a fraction, eyes dilated, body has an impulse to back away or run.
- Pain – brief in-breath followed by a long out-breath (hint of sighing) as the chest caves in a little between the shoulders, feeling the bottom lip wanting to quiver, breath starting to choke a bit.
- Anger – brief in-breath through the mouth, followed by long out-breath through the nose with gritted teeth and clenched fists, like a bull preparing to charge, a sensation of 'I'm barely holding myself back.'
- Love – this subdivides into bliss and joy (one active, one passive). Long in-breath followed by long out-breath (both through the mouth) together with a big smile, and opening the arms as if to give or receive a hug.

And finally, a mood shifter for when you're sitting at your desk feeling wound up or ground off.

Exercise: Letting go of conflict

- At the end of a long in-breath (not a short one for reasons mentioned above), tense everything up, including the fists and the face, then sigh out and (briefly) collapse.
- Repeat as needed.

- Smile, by this time next week whatever the problem is will probably be insignificant anyway.

So how does this help someone performing as a presenter, on stage or in court?

When we develop our awareness, a mindfulness about how we inhabit this body in this moment, we can use it to tame performance anxiety.

The simplest instruction under this kind of pressure? Blow out! We can then use the body's innate wisdom to bring us back to base. It works in the same way as a sigh of relief. Try one of those right now, and you'll feel the shoulders lift on the in-breath and then go down on the out-breath as the belly releases. Remember: FEAR + OXYGEN = ENERGY.

When fear strikes, the body produces adrenalin in order to fight or flee. If you don't use this energy for that purpose, it will set your mind spinning in unproductive circles. Deep breathing helps dispel resistance to this sudden energy boost (i.e. trying to act 'normal') and rebalances the mind/body split.

This may sound simplistic, but when combined with specific body-centring exercises, it is very effective. I've had people come back and thank me because they reached for it under pressure and 'it worked!'

Breath and death

Inspire: to breathe in, to create a new thought. Expire: to breathe out, to die.

This rhythm repeats over and over throughout our daily, monthly, yearly life. It is mirrored in the motion of the waves, the way night and day swap over, and how everything that comes into being, everything in the universe, also goes – be that thoughts, organisms or planets.

If the breathing is in some way limited, withheld, or constricted, so too is our interface with the world. If you believe that the world is a hostile place, then of course you won't breathe fully into it, which leaves you disempowered. Conversely, if you breathe deep and fully, you're more likely to be at home in the world.

Most people run out of breath between their ears before they do in their lungs. I experienced a graphic illustration of this in a breath workshop with the master shakuhachi flute player Riley Lee. He asked us to fully empty out our lungs then lock off the throat so no air would come in, and then wait. He told us that the impulse to wave our arms and beat our thighs would come up and that acting out that impulse would be helpful in letting go of the fierce mental imperative, 'Stop or you'll die!'

I lasted fifty seconds till I breathed in. I've never managed to reach that limit again, but sometimes I tell that story in choir when someone says, 'I'm running out of breath before the end of the line ... '

Breath and the connection with mindfulness

Mindfulness is an ancient practice that has become popular in the West as a tool for becoming more alive and available in the present. It's based on the simple act of watching your breath. I've left it till last because by now, I'm hoping you can tune into some of the rich possibilities of that simple act.

Exercise: A simple mindfulness practice

- Sit with eyes your closed, spine upright. Place the soles of your feet on the floor with the palms of your hands connected or resting on the knees.
- Slightly lengthen the in-breath, then likewise the out-breath.
- Notice how that moves the belly, ribs and shoulder blades.
- Notice how there may be a habit of holding the belly in, and release.
- Witness how thoughts come and go, taking you away from this simple activity. The monkey mind will tug at your sleeve and hassle you for your attention. Remember, your thoughts are objects; they are just thoughts.
- If possible, detach a little from the thoughts and notice that you don't have to take them so seriously, or even accept them as defining your reality.

> **TIP:** The practice of letting thoughts come and go (emphasis on the go) and sitting calm and centred in the middle of all the noise they generate makes life easier and simpler.
>
> Try combining all this with a simple daily activity, such as doing the dishes, or walking. Notice how the mind will take you into the past or the future, and the body and breath will bring you back to the present.

A YIN AND YANG OF MINDFULNESS

In recent years, large corporations have seized on mindfulness as a way of making people more efficient at work. Ideally, people who come for a technique to help them deal with multi-tasking will find something much richer in the subtleties of their relationship with their breath. Here's a practice to explore.

Exercise: Finding the full extent of your breath

- Focus on the in-breath, sending oxygen through the arteries all the way to the extremities: the toes, the fingers, and even the ear lobes.
- Tune into that sensation of inflating the body with life force, also known as chi or prana.
- Feel the outer sheath of the body expanding outwards until

the sense of where your body ends and the rest of the universe begins starts to dissolve.

When our diaphragm pulls down it creates a vacuum in our lungs that pulls the blood back from the extremities and into our lungs so that the exchange of oxygen can take place. (I thank Jack Tenen for pointing this out to me.)

The expanding sensation that the in-breath creates disguises this process, but you can do the above practice with this awareness. The dissolving happens in a gentler, subtler way, with more of a 'surrendering into' than a 'pushing outwards'.

CASE STUDY

In the early nineties I did a year-long retreat in an ashram in India. I'd discovered transcendental meditation years before and it had been a lifesaver in rescuing me from the youthful angst of chasing every thought I had down every rabbit hole to find out what it really meant.

Various spiritual teachers had said that there was much more to meditation than this, and I wanted to find the maximum, no-holds-barred, 100 per cent version. I decided that I should go the source, hence the trip to India. It was an intense, life-changing experience.

One of the adjuncts to meditation practice was a lot of full-on group therapy, run by remarkable facilitators who took us to some incredible places that I couldn't possibly have experienced otherwise. Of the groups I did, the Mt Everest version, was a two-week Primal Therapy group.

I'd heard it was intense. I'd heard that it was very physical, very cathartic, that it started before dawn and continued till bedtime. There was a special diet – no caffeine, no alcohol, no spicy food – and no talking. (Lots of yelling and screaming, though!) There was no interaction with anyone outside the group room, no music, no reading, no mirrors, no masturbation ... in other words, nowhere else to escape to. Just a sense of 'this is your life'.

As the first day approached, I could feel an inescapable tidal wave coming. I became fixated on the idea that each morning of the week before I started, I had to swim the length of the nearby swimming pool (3 metres short of Olympic length) – underwater.

I'm a lousy swimmer. Where I grew up, near Liverpool in England, the local pool was small and too crowded to swim lengths. Within seconds of standing next to it, your eyes would sting from the outgassing of chlorine, and in the industrial wasteland known as The Black Country, two centuries of industrial revolution had blighted the land. If you fell into any large, local body of water, you probably needed to be hospitalised. For some reason though, I was good at swimming underwater – although never yet 47 metres at a stretch.

Every morning as I stood at the edge of the pool, I didn't know if I could actually meet the challenge again. I took big breaths into my floating ribs and beyond, then once I'd dived, I repeated a mantra over and over that had been mentioned in meditation training: 'You are not the mind; you are not the body.'

I realised that as I reached the halfway mark, where the floor started dropping away towards the deep end, just as my mind was screaming, 'Go up or you'll die!' I had to ignore that instruction and aim downwards, otherwise the body's natural buoyancy would take over and I would inevitably be gasping at the surface. If I could pull this off, I would experience a beautiful breakthrough in which I felt I could keep going forever (or at least until the end of the pool).

Each time, after I reached that point of life and death struggle, I experienced that same wonderful breakthrough. It showed me in practice what during meditation teaching had only been a theory. It introduced me to Walt Whitman's question, 'Darest thou now O soul, Walk out with me toward the unknown region?'

It was a place that was somewhere beyond birth and death. It was a very simple, silent place. Then, as I came close to the end wall of the pool, normal life would kick in again, the imperative would insist, and I was grasping the wall with heaving lungs, half of me still underwater and half emerging back into the sounds and colours of the real world.

I tell this story to illustrate some of the illusion around how much air (life force) we have in us, and our belief in what we can or can't do. Have a big breath in and out. Go on, it's free!

IN BRIEF

- Relieve stress by coming back down to ground.
- Trim, taut and terrific stops you breathing fully.
- Breath is a means of changing mood – fear, pain, anger and love.
- Fear + Oxygen = Energy
- Breath fully, e.g. standing in the constructive rest position and press the lower back into the wall.
- Mindfulness – breath takes us on the ride through the body.

VOICE AS YOUR GATEWAY TO PERSONAL POWER 5

When you release your voice, magic happens.

This chapter shows you how to use your voice to explore your personal power. It describes an actor's secret tool, Psychological Gesture, and shows how the Stand and Deliver method is a cure for feeling like a fraud.

Most of us learned to inhibit and imprison ourselves when we made the shift from our loud and free voice (the one we howled our way into this world with), to something more restrained, cautious and careful.

One of the most obvious ways of unleashing this power we have learned to hide is to let the voice out, in whoops and hollers and yells, in song and in sobs and in full-on, side-splitting laughter.

How easy would it be for you to stand up in your living room and yell, 'Oh, yeah!' with your full voice? Would you feel silly? Would you feel like you couldn't because of the neighbours or someone else in the house?

And yet, why not do exactly that? Just for the hell of it! If we were watching a movie and the lead character stood up for themselves like that we'd cheer them on, so why wouldn't we do that for ourselves? Why would we want to keep the lid on our own power?

Most of us learned to hide our power because, for various reasons, it was too much for the big people who supervised our life. Even the most loving of parents needed to teach us to shift from our outdoor voice to our indoor one. Many parents, and relatives, struggling with their own wounds and problems, were much more stringent. My parents would remind us that they grew up in the era of children being seen and not heard. Such rigorous conditioning can be often be felt several generations later.

In over thirty years of individual sessions I've heard so many stories of psychological or actual violence at the hands of parents, teachers, siblings, step-parents and so on. We interpreted the messages we received and turned down our lights and hid our sound and our spirit in order to find safety. We 'held our tongue', we 'gritted out teeth', we 'swallowed our words' and caged our power because speaking up for ourselves had dire consequences.

I've heard many horror stories, most a variation on the theme of attack by an adult: 'Miss Jones told me to stand up at the back and just mime.' At some point, it dawned on me that it's not just what was said all those years ago, but what was perceived.

I noticed that there were two seasons in life where people

felt attacked about their voice. The first comes around age seven, when we make the shift to come out from under our mother's wing. The second coincides with the onset of puberty, roughly seven years later.

This led me to the notion that we have a certain hypersensitivity at these times and that maybe Miss Jones was just a bit harassed, or distracted that day and she said something a bit dismissive, but what was perceived was something far worse. At those ages, that hypersensitivity promotes a perverse logic based on the old notion of 'Nobody loves me.'

Of course, we will never know what actually happened, but what I do know is that voice is a remarkably responsive muscle, and that, decades later it can thaw out in a matter of minutes.

So yes, there are consequences from letting your voice out in its full power. And they can be wonderful. Clients who come for vocal sessions report back about the changes that happen in their lives. Someone quits a job: 'It was slowly killing me ...' Someone negotiates a huge raise: 'I realised I had to back myself ...' Someone else leaves an unhappy marriage: 'He's a good man, but I just couldn't stand him touching me any more ...'

Exploring these physical shifts will bring to the surface our beliefs that contradict our sense of self-worth, and this is where another form of valuable personal development starts.

Psychological Gesture: an actor's secret tool

At the end of the nineteenth century, the Russian Director Konstantin Stanislawski raised actor training to a whole new level by 'holding the mirror up to nature'. He was operating in an era when cinema was in its infancy, and psychology was a toddler, a time when many thought that scientific principles were poised to solve all the mysteries of the universe. He applied these principles to the study of acting, and devised a system, which became known as The Method, which is designed to bring as much authenticity as possible to the performed scenes and the profession.

Stanislawski's rebel pupil Vsevolod Meyerhold grew a body of work, which advanced the method by using a form of physicality. This was picked up by another Russian actor and teacher Michael Chekhov (Anton's nephew), who devised something he called Psychological Gesture.

Simply described, this technique showed actors how to reliably replicate a character or an emotion by finding the exact physical stance or gesture that would evoke those properties through a muscle memory derived from life or in rehearsal. Once the actor embodied this psychological gesture, they could use it to find themselves reliably, authentically, in character.

Decades later, Richard Bandler and John Grinder came up with a similar technique in their system of neuro-linguistic programming. They used the term 'anchoring' to describe a method whereby physical sensation is used to fix a new mental pattern into a person's belief system. In the chapter Body Language, Body Wisdom there is a reference to a Ted Talk by professor Amy Cuddy of the Harvard Business School, in which she presented a 'proof' of this phenomenon.

PSYCHOLOGICAL GESTURE AND THE SWORD OF TRUTH

The Sword of Truth is a useful tool that grew out of Psychological Gesture and is described in detail on page 42. I'm mentioning it again here because in feedback forms from training sessions people consistently cite this as one of the most useful tools they gained. It is also a means of authentically locating your power and showing it to the world, and is a very useful precursor to the coming exercise 'Stand and Deliver'.

This Sword of Truth gesture can be used while you're waiting to start your presentation or waiting your turn to speak at a round-table discussion. With your hand in your lap, you can grasp your sword firmly without anyone else noticing what's going on. This is your secret weapon, and the way it works is by using your body's strength and wisdom to hold your monkey mind steady and focused on what is useful to you, reining it in from running away with negative self-talk.

SHOW 'EM WHO YOU ARE!

When working with a client on their confidence and gravitas, I may ask them to find their Strong Stance (see page 45) with feet wide apart, arms up, shoulders down, hands reaching for the heavens. This is a platform for making bold statements. The nature of the statement varies from person to person, of course, and here's one of my favourite sequences.

- Take up a position, in Strong Stance and declare to the skies:
  'Billions of atoms came from across the universe to form me!'
  'I am a miracle of nature!'
  'I am amazing!'

So what do you think? Consider the following questions.

- What was your first reaction to reading this section?
- What was your reaction to the part (however small) that imagined standing and saying that yourself?
- Did you notice any physical sensation in response?
- Where was it located in the body?
- How many of those reactions were thoughts that in some way put a limit on you?
- Who or what would you be without those limits?
- How willing are you on a scale of 1–10 to overcome those limitations?

It may seem an outrageous statement, but if you look at it objectively, it's all true. We *are* a miracle of nature, and so is every single human on the planet – so why not declare the truth? And what about declaring aloud other truths about yourself – certainly the ones your best friends would say about you.

At the end of the chapter Voice for Presenters, I talked about networking and the importance of having a short but colourful response, scripted ahead of time, to describe what you do. When coaching people I often get them to start that script with a bold statement, and then stand up and declare it out loud.

The interesting thing is people's reactions when making such bold statements. There's often an involuntary physical reaction, even if just a subtle twitch, when the body language contradicts what's being said. Exploring these physical shifts will bring to the surface those beliefs that contradict our sense of self-worth, and this is where another form of valuable personal development starts.

I make sure that people quickly lasso the negative comments their Inner Critic makes before these thoughts can scuttle off and be embedded by the Inner Censor. Next step is to shine a light on those thoughts. Sometimes that alone is enough to show them up as invalid. Other times, more work is needed.

There is a simple process, borrowed from cognitive behaviour therapy, called Weeding and Seeding. Working with a friend or coach (or your log book,) take each one of those beliefs that are likely to shoot you down and find a clear, definite and positive answer (that you believe in) that contradicts them.

For example, 'I'm too short to be able to command this situation' becomes 'Crown on, grounded, strong as a mountain.' (See the chapter Body Language for an explanation of how Putting a Crown on Your Head and Grounding works.)

Exercise: Stand and deliver

Combine the following with the Sword of Truth and you'll be a force to be reckoned with.

- Choose a bold headline for your professional identity, e.g. a book editor might say 'I am a manuscript midwife.'
- Find three statements about your history that point to how you got there. Choose interesting ones that make the listener want to ask more about it, e.g. 'I won a Churchill scholarship to study how they do this in Transylvania' rather than simply, 'I did an MBA.'
- Choose something different, unusual, quirky, about how you got there, probably something more personal than professional. This last part is not essential to the process, but can give you the confidence to back yourself on the main ones.
- Rehearse your script (not too long of course), and when you're ready, stand up and deliver these statements to the world.

- Catch any line of negative self-talk and ask yourself, 'Is that true?' Usually it isn't, or it may only be partially true. Use Weeding and Seeding to help rearrange this belief. If it's persistent then take the problem and magnify it, dramatise it, exaggerate it – in other words, don't take yourself too seriously.
- Deliver again till you dare to speak boldly and loudly, or calmly and matter-of-factly.

Impostor Syndrome

It's time to talk about Impostor Syndrome. A term coined in 1978 by clinical psychologists Dr Pauline Clance and Suzanne Imes, it refers to the inability of some high-achieving individuals to internalise their accomplishments and their persistent fear of being exposed as a fraud.

Working as an executive coach is an extraordinary privilege – you get a glimpse into the fears and doubts that lurk beneath so many people's professional personas. Indeed, if a relationship of trust has been built with a client (and without that there may not be much value in the coaching), you start to notice that people share the same basic negative beliefs about their work, regardless of professional or personal background.

In the privacy of their own head, when they step into the shower in the morning, it may take on many versions, but they all boil down to the same one: 'I'm not good enough for this project/promotion/position/team.' A lot of the time this is not based on fact, but a mood or a habit. The result can poison your working day and waste big chunks of your life.

If this sounds in any way familiar, believe me, you are not alone. But there is an antidote to these dark, hidden thoughts – shine a light on them and often the dark part fades, or at the very least, shrinks.

In their research, Imes and Clance looked at the professional behaviours of high-achieving women with Impostor Syndrome. In 1993, Clance conceded that Impostor Syndrome was not a uniquely female problem, since 'males in these populations are just as likely as females to have low expectations of success and to make attributions to non-ability related factors'.

The key behaviours of Impostor Syndrome observed were:

- Diligence – gifted people often work hard to prevent others from discovering that they are so-called impostors. This hard work often leads to more praise and success, which perpetuates the impostor feelings and fears of being found out. The individual may feel they need to work two or three times as hard so they over-prepare, tinker and obsess over details. This can lead to burn-out and sleep deprivation.
- Feelings of being phony – those with impostor feelings often try to give supervisors and teachers the answers that they

believe they want, which often leads to an increase in the feeling that they're being fake.
- Use of charm – professionally gifted women may use their intuitive perceptiveness and charm to gain approval and praise from supervisors. Moreover, charm is deployed to seek out relationships with supervisors to help the woman increase intellectual and creative opportunities. Interestingly, when praise or recognition is given by a supervisor, the woman infers that this is based on her charm and not on ability.
- Avoiding displays of confidence – another way that a person can perpetuate their impostor feelings is to avoid showing any confidence in their abilities. Specifically, this person may think that if they actually believe in their intelligence and abilities, they will be rejected by others. Therefore, they may convince themselves that they are not intelligent or don't deserve success, simply to avoid this possibility.

> **TIP:** You can try the processes I've described above on your own and it will definitely reap benefits if you persist, but the nature of those dark shameful bits is that we desperately want to avoid them. To fully commit to this technique, you will need a coach or a wise, capable friend to hold you to account.

CASE STUDY

Amanda is a highly successful owner of a coaching and training business and is used to standing in front of a room full of people as a lead presenter.

A few years ago she discovered she could sing, and this had a profound effect on her life. She remembers her mother saying when she was younger, 'Don't sing, dear ... You're very flat, love ... Such a pity that you're tone deaf.' She also remembers one of her daughters kicking the back of her car seat with, 'Mum, stop singing!'

We met at an organisational psychologists' conference where I was coming in at the end of the first day to bring the room full of people together by getting them to sing. Amanda remembers we started out the session with calls and whoops and hollers and thinking this was fun and non-threatening. Before long that afternoon, she was one of a group of fifty people singing a simple three-part harmony.

This experience showed Amanda that she did actually have a singing voice, and gave her the urge to sing more, so she enrolled in the Soulsong choir. When the day came to go to her first choir meeting, her Inner Censor came to the fore, so she emailed me and Michel, the choir's administrator, to warn us that she couldn't sing and to check whether she should come or not. Of course, we encouraged her to come and within minutes of arriving, Amanda found she was having fun doing the warm-up sounds and before long, she was doing fine, singing with the choir.

The next breakthrough came doing a Singing Solo workshop with me. When she stood up to sing to a small group of people, Amanda went blank and couldn't sing while seeing the seven faces in front of her. I got her to lie back on some nearby pillows and imagine she was in the bath. This unlocked her voice, and out it came, easy and free. She came out of that threshold experience with the feeling, 'Well, if I can do that lying down, I can do it standing up.'

After doing it standing up, performing solo in front of a room of ninety people some time later, Amanda thought, 'If I can do that, I can do anything!' She felt it was so much fun that it was like having a new toy to play with any time she wanted.

One major payoff that Amanda noticed is the removal of fears that previously cropped up in her professional life. When she was working as a trainer and facilitator, despite years of experience and feeling relatively confident out front, there was always a quota of negative self-talk that had to be pushed aside and overcome. She now noticed that her Inner Perfectionist wasn't allowed to run the show any more.

Amanda's thoughts shifted. 'What I am is a human being on a journey, I'm here to enjoy and experiment. I'm stepping through from censoring to acceptance, and acknowledging that it's okay to be myself. I don't have to get it right all the time. Being a human who is learning and experimenting is more powerful than trying to have all the answers.'

She has also said, 'When I'm coaching people now, I'm more able to tell them, "Just start with what you've got"; I'm speaking from experience.' She talks of how this experience of voice work has taken away most of that normal everyday angst that many people hardly notice because it's been there so long. It has been replaced with feeling comfortable in her own skin.

Amanda's second breakthrough came when she did the Singing Solo *course again, a few years later. This time we worked on her voice to find some rich, lower resonances. She'd asked for this because she'd noticed that when she got enthusiastic about a topic (especially on the phone) her voice went very high, and she was likely to lose her credibility.*

A big shift happened when I asked her to show off. The key was for her to give herself permission to unashamedly go for her radiant source of energy. When she found a deeper, stronger connection between her voice and her belly, she found a much more resonant, weightier voice.

She notes that this earthier voice also helps her come back to an awareness of being in the moment without the pollution of her inner critic telling her she should be somehow different from how she is being right now.

IN BRIEF

- Find the ingredients that sharpen your Sword of Truth.
- Make bold statements from your strong stance.
- Develop the authentic story of yourself that you can deliver boldly.
- Discuss with your colleagues which version of the Impostor Phenomenon they're most susceptible to. Shining a light on this common ailment helps loosen its grip.

WOMEN'S VOICE: THE QUIET REVOLUTION   6

This chapter deals with women speaking out in the workplace and explores the balance between assertiveness and aggressiveness. It looks at common pitfalls for women who need to speak out, and how to avoid them.

As a man speaking on behalf of women, I know I'm sticking my neck out in telling them how to raise their voice, so before anyone gets a noose out, let me explain how I got here.

Four out of five people who come to see me for individual voice sessions are female. Additionally, for a few years now I've been co-facilitating a corporate program called 'As She Speaks' with Mary Ferguson, which aims to help women crack the glass ceiling. There are certain issues that I see constantly arising for women, and given my history I feel I can be of use here.

I grew up in a house full of strong women, amongst the 'satanic mills' in coal and steel country in the north of England. In this industrial landscape gender roles were well defined. Dad was a shift worker so we didn't see much of him. Both my sisters were academically very bright, but when my older sister looked like being the first child in our neighbourhood to go to university, Dad was sceptical about it for a while. A woman's place was looking after the home and the kids. Later in life when that same sister's male partner became one of the first fully transgender women in England, it was decided (for his own benefit) to keep Dad in the dark about it.

When I first came to Australia on tour with a theatre group, I had the good fortune to be given a female part. In rehearsal I had many insights into how much harder my life would be if I wasn't walking around in a tall, white, middle-class body, and at the same time, understood some of the benefits of inhabiting (as best I could) a female consciousness.

Having crossed between these polarities, I saw how much of my upbringing had sent me towards an appreciation of the female end of the spectrum. The binary definition of gender and its requirement to conform to type is dissolving fast, and I'm excited to realise that I can let go of some of my inherited definitions of maleness. The upcoming generation is more open to seeing themselves as somewhere on a spectrum between male and female. For those who need help getting a handle on that, the January 2017 edition of *National Geographic*, 'Gender Revolution', devotes an excellent issue to a worldwide study of this topic.

All this helps me understand how I came to be on a mission championing the cause of women; partly because I think the world would be a better place with more of a balance of power between yin and yang and, if nothing else, for the benefit of those female qualities that live in me.

The balance of power

Consider the following statistics:

- How many examples are there of any woman being the head of a national newspaper or TV station? Whoever does the requisite research on this would have to come up with a very small number, and yet these are the major vehicles by which a society speaks to itself, even in an age where they are threatened by a take-over from social media.
- The 2016 Fortune 500 list includes just 21 companies with women at the helm, down from 24 in 2014. Or, to look at it another way, women now hold a paltry 4.2 per cent of CEO positions in America's 500 biggest companies.
- There are only nine female Australian CEO's in ASX 200 companies (less than men named John).
- In 2013, the Abbot government in Australia had only one woman in the cabinet. Perhaps some of his female supporters could see nothing wrong with the fact that he nominated himself as minister for women.
- When Hilary Clinton was defeated by Barack Obama in her first electoral race, one commentator remarked, 'America could cope with electing a black man before it could cope with a woman.'

I'm citing these issues to point out that, to many people, this imbalance has been the state of affairs for so long that it appears normal.

The good news

An increasing number of companies are acknowledging the fact that there's a gender imbalance at the top of the hierarchy, and many have set diversity programs in place. More and more of their clients want to know that they will be looked after by women, or that they aren't just dealing with the old boys' club.

In 2012 researchers at the The Columbia Business School analysed data from the top 1500 companies in America, from 1992 to 2006, to determine the relationship between companies' performances and female participation in senior management. Firms that had women in top positions performed better.

Since the global financial crisis, it's become clear; more women around means fewer pointless risks. What used to be a marker of leadership – the ability to act quickly and remain in a state of pumped up confidence – was recast as a liability. At the same time characteristics regarded as examples of feminine weakness – hesitating, waiting for outside feedback and confirmation – now show up as clear thinking and good management. The movie *The Wolf of Wall Street* demonstrated in agonising detail how horribly wrong things can go when fuelled by testosterone surges.

I'm not saying that significant changes will happen overnight, but if the journey of a thousand miles begins with a single step, then even just shining a light of awareness on these topics already takes you a chunk of the distance.

This is a 'quiet' revolution because there are no obvious signs of blood in the streets, no assassination of dictators, and because it's been gradual (some say agonisingly slow). Sometimes it's been a case of three steps forward, two steps back. At the time of writing, America has elected an old, white, anti-feminist male. The step forward is that it brought millions of women worldwide out onto the street in protest and solidarity. If these are the outer circumstances holding women back, what internal conditions contribute to it?

Fear of being 'too much'

When I first moved to Australia, I started teaching voice in Sydney's Blackwattle Bay Studio. In the previous four years I'd been working in Holland where space is at a premium, and to me the upstairs floor of this old warehouse seemed vast. To communicate from one corner to another was far enough to warrant shouting, which turned out to be a useful circumstance for tricking people into using a powerful, projecting, calling voice. When the situation demands that we use our biggest voice – I sometimes use the example of hollering for a taxi – our body knows what to do. Most people did it quite naturally as a child.

The technique worked successfully for weeks until one day, a woman named Jeannette was hollering across the studio. Suddenly she stopped, closed her mouth, stepped back and denied she'd done it. There was such a strong disconnect between what she was saying and what she'd actually done, that I had to find out why.

The act of standing up and hollering makes the strong statement, 'Stop what you're doing and listen to me!' This implies boldness, high status, and a fearless cry that you're now top dog, with all the implications and consequences that carries too.

It put me in mind of reliving a battle cry, and I realised that for women, throughout history, a battle cry usually meant suffering and subjection. Half the world was (and in some places still is) in slavery, be that for an Asian farmworker or a woman with a mink. She must behave, be submissive. To be forthright, independent and to speak out once meant being burnt at the stake. In many instances today, a woman may be accused of being 'shrill' or a 'ball-busting bitch' when perhaps the same actions from a man might be called 'assertive'. I've often heard it said that, for women, finding the right balance here is as tricky as a tightrope walk, however, I would suggest that despite the misogyny it invokes, if more women take the risk of being 'too much', more men will eventually get used to it.

I certainly hope that Jeannette may by now have done more voice lessons and developed her capacity for projection, and felt her body vibrate with the power of her own voice. I hope she feels the tingle of freedom when she takes the lid off her magnificence.

CASE STUDY

Jennifer was in her late twenties and a lawyer who had moved across to HR. After a while she confessed she felt safer in that department. Our first meeting was over the phone, and I was struck by how young and girlish her voice sounded.

We worked together on her finding her Power Sound. It was a bold move for her to be standing on the thirtieth floor of a glass and concrete tower overlooking the Sydney Opera House and to make big sounds that might conceivably be heard by her colleagues on the same floor.

I asked her to wave and call out a long 'Hello-o-o-o' to an imaginary friend sitting on the roof of the Opera House. Jennifer was shocked by the power of her own voice, and at first wanted to shy away from it. After a while, she identified that she was a little confronted by the changes she would inevitably make in her life if she really followed this path of freedom. Needless to say, her phone voice has already changed.

WHERE THE CHANGE BEGAN

You could say, for instance, it started a century ago with the suffragette movement, however it's still in living memory that women had no voice in business, media or government. If you saw them there they were most likely taking shorthand or making the tea.

In the sixties and seventies the pill, the single mother's pension, plus the Baby Boomers' lust for freedom were part of the growth of feminism. Germaine Greer wrote *The Female Eunuch* and singer/songwriters like Carole King and Joni Mitchell took hold of the microphone. They let the world know a woman's point of view on sex, love and what it was like for her the morning after a one-night stand. The journey of self-discovery, self-disclosure and of taking over the reins had begun.

Women made many valuable inroads into male-dominated professions. Now girls growing up in the West could go to school on an equal footing, and now there were co-ed schools where they could also be friends with boys. When I taught at Monash University it was common knowledge among undergraduates that women could even average better grades, although a common response in discussion about this issue would go something like, 'We're all equal now.'

It seemed to me that because some of the young women had no experience to compare it with, they tended to regard those struggles as ancient history, not realising that a battle half-won could also easily be lost. We still live in a world where males in power might want to outlaw abortion, or jail a Saudi woman for driving a car, or even throw acid in the face of a girl who dares to go to school. Australia has recently woken up to the disturbing statistics on domestic violence; how an alarming number of women risk being beaten or even murdered by their partner for speaking up for themselves. My step-daughter is petite and no expert at martial arts. She is in much more danger of rape than her male counterparts.

In books and film we love to cheer the underdog. Hollywood is particularly fond of the story that anyone can live his or her dream, despite apparently insurmountable odds, and become a star or a president.

If half the world is female and therefore qualifies for 'underdog' status (why does this sound condescending in this paragraph but not in the previous one?), the times are calling for a redress of this imbalance. How many of those women graduates who regard themselves as equal still have a knee-jerk impulse to say 'sorry' way more often than their male counterparts? How many female law students do the stats and notice that while 58 per cent of law graduates are women, 80 per cent of barristers are men? (To be fair to the legal profession, it is waking up to the fact that having more female partners will be good for the bottom line and flexible working hours make the workplace more user-friendly to parents, predominantly women.)

Conversely, Community Music Victoria has about 850 choirs on its books. Their members are predominantly women. Statistics are hard to track, but 80 per cent female participation is normal for a community choir. In individual voice sessions I conduct, the ratio is about the same. Here the situation seems reversed. The older ('me') generation of men seem to be shyer about developing their singing voice. From my standpoint as a vocal coach it's tempting to see this as part of the quiet revolution. Women are looking for, and finding their voice. A choir is a safe place to do that.

WHAT THIS MEANS IN PRACTICE

First let's tackle the 'S' word, the one that women use much more than men.

Recently, when the tram I was standing on came to a sudden stop, I accidentally stepped on a woman's foot, and she said 'Sorry.' For many women, this word means an array of things, including 'Can I have your attention?' or 'That's not right.'

On one occasion when Mary Ferguson and I were conducting an 'As She Speaks' seminar for a global law firm, the head of HR, a feisty woman, who seemed to have no problem speaking her mind to men, said, 'Our department is almost entirely women, and I see no problem with saying sorry, it's like a conversational tag, a normal part of a conversation.'

She was a bit sceptical when I pointed out that although it worked fine between women, for men (unless they are delivering an apology) it usually means, 'I am somehow less than you, I'm acknowledging my lower status.' This is a bit of a crude translation, but you get the picture. It's a variation on one of those humorous 'Mars and Venus' lists where on one side is what one gender speaks and the other side what the other gender hears.

> **TIP:** When the impulse to say sorry comes up, try replacing it with, 'Excuse me.' This allows a lot more nuance, doesn't have to sound like an apology, and in fact can be delivered with an authoritative tone.

CASE STUDY
Some years ago, I tested this theory in a seminar when a young and petite Vietnamese lawyer said, 'My boss is only small, but when she walks into the room everyone follows her. How does she do that?'

I asked her to give the other people in the room a series of simple random instructions, for instance moving someone from one chair to another. My instructions to her were secret; I asked her to first preface each of these instructions with the word 'sorry', then to repeat the exercise using 'excuse me' instead. Many participants didn't actually realise what she had done differently, but everyone noted there was 'so much more authority the second time!'

The thorny issue of status

In training sessions when I bring up the issue of status and move people into practical exercises to deal with the issue (some of which are outlined in the chapter Body Language Body Wisdom) some people are disturbed by it. Mostly it seems they would rather not open this box because they were happier believing that ours is a largely classless society. When I throw gender into the mix in the context of status, that really turns the heat up. 'So you think that in order to be successful women have to act like men!?' is what I often hear. The answer is, most definitely not. I would far rather live in a society that isn't run by alpha males, you know; the ones who invaded Iraq and gave us the Global Financial Crisis ... I point out that while women don't have to act like alpha men, they do need to be aware of their language, and to be aware of the signals they're giving off in terms of eye contact and body language.

Advice from a woman of the world

At this point I'd like to call on a friend and colleague and people whisperer, Anneli Blundell, who can speak with more authority on this topic than I can.

I would add that Anneli is a living answer to those who say, 'Well, because I'm short, people don't notice me.' She is petite yet unafraid to take command. I've seen her move into a discussion circle of tall men standing networking, and it's quite clear she's a peer amongst her equals.

Here's what she has learned from her experience, having coached professionally senior women for the past ten years to increase their visibility, authority and presence in the workplace.

THREE WAYS WOMEN MINIMISE THEIR POWER (AND HOW TO STOP)

Women are guilty of abusing their power, but not in the way they think: women abuse their power by minimising it. Specifically, there are three ways that women commonly avoid their power: Denying, Downplaying and Doubting.

1. Denying

We confuse the people we are leading by denying the power inherent in an assigned role. As leaders, we are looked to by others to make decisions, set standards and give feedback. When we don't act accordingly – because we don't feel qualified – people don't know where they stand and can wonder why we're reluctant to lead.

Consider:

- 'I don't deserve this.'
- 'Others are more skilled; I just got lucky.'
- 'I was in the right place at the right time.'

> **TIP:** View yourself through the eyes of others, and let their faith in you build your confidence. Act as if you deserve to be leading: faking confidence can build confidence. Model your behaviour other leaders who embrace their power, and use it for the good of others.

2. Downplaying

When we are naturally good at something, we tend to underestimate our ability and downplay our strengths: if it's easy for us, it must be easy for others. Downplaying our efforts, combined with a general reluctance to brag means we perpetuate the likelihood of being passed over by others who confidently promote their potential and step fully into their power.

Consider:

- 'It was nothing.'
- 'We all worked on it together.'
- 'Anyone could have done it.'

3. Doubting

Consider:

- 'I'm not sure I'm experienced enough to do this.'
- 'Who am I to be leading this team?'
- 'When will they realise I'm an impostor?'

And the solution:

- Rejoice in your doubt, knowing that it's a sign of your capability.
- Fake it to make it: confidence comes from doing the things at which you're not confident. To build confidence, you must act with confidence.

- Do more of what scares you most.

To counter this, make a list of skills, attributes and traits of which you can be proud. It's important to acknowledge these strengths to yourself. Now practise telling people what you are proud of achieving and why (in a way that doesn't make you squirm!). Try responding to compliments with a simple, 'Thank you.' This forces you to own your power and not deny it.

CASE STUDY

I was called into a global firm of management consultants. They had quite a diversity of cultures represented and I was asked to work with Alia, a Turkish woman who was brilliant at analysis and leading her team. However, her upbringing made her deferential among the (mostly male) partners. When I sat in on a meeting she had with one of the (male) partners, her body language was very telling. As he entered the meeting she went to shake his hand, but was so obviously deferential that her head quite definitely tipped and her gaze dropped.

We worked on hollering and some of the techniques outlined in the chapter Body Language, Body Wisdom to develop her Strong Stance and therefore her self-confidence.

Months later she gleefully reported back that a couple of the men asked her what she'd done that was different. One of them actually asked her if she'd started going to the gym!

WORDS THAT, SORT OF, LET YOU DOWN

In her book *How to Say it for Women*, Phyllis Mindell talks about women use a language of submissiveness. One of her pet hates is what she calls Puny Hedges. She's drawing awareness to the way our use of language can let us down. (This, of course, refers to men too.)

Hedges are a way of softening our message, letting people know that we're really a nice person after all. Examples include:

- 'You shouldn't really do that …'
- 'I'd sort of like to get that promotion …'
- 'I guess …'
- 'I just …'
- 'I feel …'
- 'I'm not sure how strongly I feel about this, but …'
- 'I guess my question is …
- 'I'm not an expert on that, but …'
- 'I don't know anything about financial reports, but …'

She goes on to offer alternatives such as:

- *Puny hedge:* You shouldn't really curse on the job.
  Assertion: Cursing at work offends people.
- *Puny hedge:* I'd sort of like to get that promotion …
  Assertion: Please consider my promotion.

Alternative: The promotion will benefit the whole department.
- *Puny hedge:* In my opinion, this project will work better if we bid on each part of the job separately.
Assertion: This project will work better if we bid on each part of the job separately.

Now I'm aware that a powerful person of either gender could pull these off with aplomb, but the word is … watch out! Soraya L Chemaly, writing in *Role Reboot*, says:

> *In fifth grade I won the school courtesy prize, in other words, I won an award for being polite. My brother, on the other hand was considered class comedian. Globally, childhood politeness lessons are asymmetrical. We socialise girls to take turns, listen carefully, not curse, and resist interrupting, in ways we do not expect boys to do.*

She goes on to detail how common it is for her to be condescended to, or interrupted by, a man, and in closing says,

> *In general I'm loath to take the approach that girls should be responsible for the world's responses to them, but I say practice these words every day:*
> *Stop interrupting me.*
> *I just said that.*

No explanation needed.
It will do both boys and girls a world of good, and no small number of adults too.

Finally, if you're a man and you're still reading this chapter I'm assuming you're on side here, so I'll suggest that we need to spread the word among our colleagues. We have a responsibility to speak out against sexism in its many and subtle forms. Many of us want to know that our daughters will operate in a world of equal opportunity.

Indeed, I recently overheard a high-ranking female executive weighing in on a debate her male colleagues were having about quotas for hiring women into higher-ranking jobs. She said something along the lines of, 'Not another presentation about the need for diversity in the firm, not another survey on unconscious bias, just frickin' do it!'

IN BRIEF

- Replace the 'S' word with 'Excuse me.'
- Women minimise their power by Denying, Downplaying and Doubting. Make a list of attributes you're proud of and tell people about them.
- Beware of 'hedge words'.

SINGING: HOW TO IMPROVE 7

Does singing ever arouse passionate joy or sadness somewhere in you? Did you know that speaking is an extension of singing?

The next four chapters pass on techniques that professional singers use to non-professional lovers of song. After an introduction about the health benefits of singing, it outlines the three areas of the throat that can enhance your sound and describes how to access four of the six qualities of the Estill Voice Technique and describes the physical and emotional benefits of singing.

We can all make music

We have an amazing musical instrument inside us. We don't have to take it out of its case, we didn't have to buy it, and no burglar can steal it from us. Within seconds it can transport us back to remembering the intense sensation of falling in love, or a childhood memory, or feel our bodies twitch with the muscle memory of dancing to that tune.

The benefits of singing together for wellness include:

- increased lung capacity
- oxygenation of the body
- reduced blood pressure and cortisol levels
- drastically increased oxytocin and endorphin levels
- increased left/right brain hemisphere connection
- an antidote for loneliness and isolation.

The anatomy of why singing feels good

When we sing we breathe deeper, which means engaging our lower lungs. This part of us is often neglected in our sitting-at-a-desk culture, and tends to collapse our torso forward and compress the lower lungs. However, when we fully engage with singing, we stand and pump our lungs, and the core belly muscles grouped around the navel work the pump.

As previously mentioned, this core shares its location with your hara (the area at the centre of your belly as it is known in Japanese medical tradition and martial art), and your centre of gravity. If you want an illustration of what that means, try blowing up an imaginary balloon with one hand on your navel and you'll feel a strong pushing pulse from below.

Committing to singing engages so many different muscle groups in the torso that it can act like a work-out. I've had people come up to me after a choir session and say something like, 'I feel like I've been to the gym, but it's more fun!'

To give one small example, while the belly muscles work the lower lungs, up on top, your SCMs (sternocleidomastoid muscles – those that connect your collarbone to your skull just under the ear), will be lifting your sternum to create more room in the rib cage. In the meantime, your latissimus dorsi squeeze around your shoulder blades to flex the top of your lungs, while your quadratus lumborum muscles are doing something similar – and that's only part of it.

> **TIP:** To experience how a single breath can create a mood shift, imagine taking in the fragrance of your first coffee of the day, or your favourite drink, with a long in-breath. And you'll feel the lift.

Meanwhile, on the biochemical level of our body, a study by the UK Heart Foundation established that singing heartily can reduce our blood pressure and cortisol levels, the stress-coping hormone.

Clearly singing increases oxygenation, and it also increases our feel-good hormones – oxytocin and endorphin. At the same time, MRI scans show that sustained musical activity enlarges the corpus callosum, which connects the hemispheres of our brain, making an increased and harmonious connection between those left and right sides.

Neuroscience is also exploring how singing affects memory. There have been dramatic results in dealing with catatonic dementia patients. When their offspring plug them into an iPod with a specially made playlist of favourite songs from their youth, they suddenly come alive, sing, gesticulate, and even hold a conversation afterwards. For those of us not yet ready for the old folks' home, memorising the notes and lyrics of songs is as effective as Sudoku and crossword puzzles.

How our ears listen

We perceive sounds primarily by way of the ear. In the cochlea, there is an array of tiny cilia (hairs with nerve endings) that respond to the entering sound waves. Some respond to high frequencies and some to lower ones.

These tiny nerve endings send messages to different parts of the brain. The perception of music connects the auditory and motor functions, and connects the right and left hemispheres of the brain, which is why, instinctively, music with a beat makes us want to move in response.

THE THREE THROATS

First, a (very) brief intro to how the larynx produces sound. If you trace your finger from your chin down your throat, soon you'll feel a small hard notch that is the top of your thyroid cartilage. This acts as a small shield, protecting your larynx. Behind it, sitting in your windpipe are your vocal folds (historically misnamed 'vocal cords'). These are a wonderfully complex set of muscles, shaped like a pair of lips, that can pulse at hundreds of times per second, thus making sound. The body picks up this sound and amplifies it, using various resonant air chambers, such as the lungs and sinus cavities, which act like the box on a guitar, enhancing and reverberating the initial, smaller sound.

> **TIP:** On YouTube, search 'vocal folds in action', and this will show you how they operate. (Warning: this is not for the squeamish.)

Most people come into this world with a free, open voice and then life happens.

In other words, various shocks and traumas make us 'grit our teeth', 'swallow our words', or 'bite back our anger'. All these metaphors indicate constrictions that happen, from our lips to our larynx, and take away our natural sound. Here are some exercises to help re-access that freer sound.

1. The lower throat

I use this exercise for those who want an authentic, deeper tone when I'm introducing people to their 'gospel' sound.

Above your vocal folds are your false, or vestibular, vocal folds: two pieces of cartilage joined by a hinge, which acts as a second line of defence, after your epiglottis, to stop food from going into your lungs. In childhood these are very flexible, but like most muscles, if you don't use 'em you lose 'em.

They have very little to do with the actual formation of sound in normal use. (Except in Mongolian/Tuvan throat singing and the 'screamo' technique of heavy metal.) If your voice is limited only to speaking and doesn't get much opportunity to sing, yell, holler or cry, they will slowly contract until they sit there like a couple of heavy wet blankets on the free action of your sound.

- Gently hold your thumb and forefinger around the windpipe, just above the larynx.
- Do a silent giggle on an out-breath with a closed mouth – you should feel your windpipe expand downwards and outwards a little.
- Once you've established where the action is, take your hand away. If you activate this expansion of the false folds, there will be little or no sound when you breathe strongly in and out.

> **TIP:** You don't want to try to giggle every time you sing, so the way to access it easily is to incorporate it into mimicking the onset of a yawn (without actually yawning). This will give you a voice sounding like the village idiot, with that characteristic sound that escapes when we yawn. It's good practice for those who feel they need a voice that's lower, but don't want to artificially force the voice down. Essential for singing The Blues.

2. The middle throat (back of the tongue)

This is for those who hear a slightly 'choked' sound when they sing.

- Stick the tongue as far out as possible. (Think licking an ice cream that's almost out of reach.)
- Make a 'BLAAAH' sound of disgust. Use a bit of attitude.
- Run the tongue all the way around the gums, including behind the back molars.
- Take hold of both sides of your tongue and gently pull it out, making a few baby sounds. If it slips away from your fingers use a tissue or a washcloth.
- Mimic the onset of a yawn, this time focusing on allowing the tongue to drop down and forward.

If you've ever had to hold your tongue or swallow rubbish you don't really believe in, if you've ever clapped your hand over your mouth, trying to take back what you said, these metaphors have a physical manifestation: the base of the tongue contracts. This is a large and powerful muscle. It may take work to counteract bad habits.

> **TIP:** Once again, the quick way into this is to mimic the onset of a yawn, this time with the awareness of expanding the gap between the back of the tongue and the roof of the mouth. The back of the tongue drops down and forward as it does when you say, 'Yyyyeah'.

3. The top of the throat

This is of most concern to people who want confident, high notes when they sing.

- Run a finger backwards along the cleft in the roof of the mouth until you feel the bone of the skull turn to soft rubbery muscle. Stop before you hit the gag reflex. (Yes, that is possible.) This is your soft palate or velar port.
- Gently push up so that you can feel just where it is.
- Another way to feel it is to say the word 'car', on an in-breath,

and you'll get a bit of a cold minty sensation where the soft palate is.
- Now you've located it, lift it. One way is to imagine you could push your upper back molars apart. Test it by singing the word 'air' as you climb up the scale. If you've really found how to lift it, you'll be able to smooth out the gear change that happens in the join between so-called 'head' voice and 'chest' voice.

Like many muscles, it was flexible when you came into this world but then life and gravity took over and it may sag. Take heart, this is an easy one to discover and will make a drastic difference to your sound.

> **TIP:** If you need a bit more lift, try flaring your nostrils as if trying to get away from a bad smell. This may help.

The Estill Training System

As far as I can tell, no-one has yet superseded the Estill Voice Training system for its breadth and depth of exploration and the assistance it has given singers.

Jo Estill was an American singer and researcher who started studying vocal science in the early seventies, and in 1991 founded Estill Voice Training Systems for a uniform certification of instructors. Her pioneering work with X-rays of the larynx in action (laryngeal fibre endoscopy combined with a stroboscope), meant that she could give very specific information about the incredibly complex activities of the intricate muscle systems that activate as we use our voice.

She was by all accounts a very demanding teacher, but asked no more than she expected of herself:

> *Jo is so committed to uncovering the mysteries of the voice that she agreed to have 12 needles inserted in her mouth, throat, and voice musculature. To make the readings accurate, she refused anaesthetic. It was the first time and only time this research has been done.*
> Richard Lipton, Jo Estill Honorary Doctorate Oration, 2004

Estill famously identified six vocal qualities: speech, falsetto, cry, twang, opera and belting. I'll be describing the first four of these – I wouldn't attempt to introduce you to opera and belting qualities by describing them in a book.

When I tried to study this technique from books and diagrams, I quickly got bogged down in a mass of detail. Ultimately, I was led into this work by a wonderful teacher named Valerie Tamblyn-Mills, who had a 3D model of a human head that she could take apart like a jigsaw puzzle. Finally, I could make sense of the diagrams.

Suffice to say I don't think you can get very far studying this from a book without help from a teacher. Having said that, if you want to explore this work but can't afford the time or money commitment, there is one excellent book I would recommend: *Singing and the Actor* by Gillyanne Kayes.

You need a good teacher who can guide you through the anatomical details, without leaving you blinded by science. I have heard of teachers who don't really know how to make this come alive and off the page into practice, so if you are going to study this course, choose carefully – it's intense.

Despite all that, I may be able to help you discover some possibilities in your voice that may have been lying dormant.

TWANG

In sessions, once we've established an applicable breathing pattern (see Breath: Our Constant Companion on page 100) and retracted the false folds, I usually start with twang.

If you don't know how to turn that on and off, you haven't left base camp yet. There are two kinds of twang. The one to eliminate is nasal twang, which works well with Aussie drawl. This usually comes from a locked jaw and tongue, which means that your sound can't escape through your mouth so it has to exit through your nose. I do quite a bit of work in sessions helping people to remove that one if possible and discuss this further in 'Anatomical obstacles' on page 10.

Oral twang is the useful one. It activates the occipital air pockets in your skull (the place where you feel pressure drop in your ears on-board a plane). Your body is full of air pockets, the most familiar being your lungs and sinus cavities. These resonators act like the box on a guitar or violin in that they pick up the sound made by the vocal folds and amplify it.

Twang is that sharp edge around your vocal sound that helps your voice project across distance. Kids have it for free when they whinge or holler 'Muuuuuum!' Actors have to know it or they won't make themselves heard in a large auditorium. Teachers need it or they'll have chronic throat problems.

Some people are a bit scared of this sound; women especially tend to discard it as ugly or hard. This is perhaps because there are consequences from raising your voice. It is a piercing sound that says, 'Listen to me!'

I sometimes have to trick people into finding it. For example, look out the window as far into the distance as possible and call, 'Hey!' to an imagined person in the distance.

Often that's all it takes, the belly muscles kick in to power the breath, the mouth widens in a hint of a smile, the false folds retract, the back of the tongue lifts slightly, the thyroid cartilage tilts and a bright piercing sound comes out, without your conscious awareness of all that muscular adjustment.

Now take that 'Hey' sound and draw it out long, so that you're singing, 'Haaaaair' on a long breath. Because this is a very efficient breath-to-sound ratio, most people can manage to last fifteen seconds in this loud sound.

Because this sound uses a raised larynx, you may find that you lose twang as you come down to lower notes. Be patient – it is possible to combine the two.

> **TIP:** Make sure there's no rasping or tickling in the throat or undue feeling of pressure in the head. These sensations are a clear indication to back off, to lower either your pitch or volume and find out which part of your throat is restricting.

SOB/CRY

This is useful for a crooning sound, and Elvis impersonators have found this one invaluable.

- Practise your siren sound by closing the tongue against the soft palate with the sound 'NGGG'. Now slide up and down your range making a sound like a siren. This will lower your larynx.
- Opening up the gap between your tongue and soft palate again, retract the false folds, and try a little puppy whimper.
- With retracted folds and low (onset of a yawn) larynx, cry 'poor me' with your whimper voice, then keeping the false

folds well retracted, bring the 'poor me' down in pitch, with a sobbing quality.
- As you reach the bottom of your range, sing a phrase of your chosen croon. You'll notice a breathy quality, possibly including vibrato.

VIBRATO

This is the wave, or pulsing sound, most often associated with classical technique as the note varies slightly up and down in pitch and/or volume. As a personal taste, I like it best used in moderation, especially by those singers who can bring vibrato into the latter half of a note to make it warm and give it shimmer.

As an ex working-class English boy, for years I believed opera was culturally unacceptable, that it was posh and for snobs. Later in life I fell in love with various bits of opera and realised what a rich tradition I was cutting myself off from, but I still find an overdone vibrato hard to listen to.

In the history of singing it's a relative newcomer; Renaissance music preferred a simpler, purer sound. In Baroque times, it was often used quite exaggeratedly as ornamentation. In the Anglo-Germanic world it was often regarded as a Latin affectation.

When Enrico Caruso made his acclaimed New York Metropolitan Opera debut in November 1903, one of the specific vocal attributes for which he was praised by music reviewers was the absence of a disruptive vibrato from his singing. The scholarly critic William James Henderson wrote in *The Sun* newspaper that Caruso 'has a pure tenor voice and [it] is without the typical Italian bleat.'

I have helped people discover their vibrato, but I won't attempt to describe that process here without doing it as part of a session.

> **TIP:** Having said that, with a couple of people I've said, 'How would you make a fake opera sound?' I then asked them how would it sound if they did it in a relaxed way and bingo! There was their vibrato.

FALSETTO

This is a breathy tone that at high pitches stretches the vocal folds long and tight. In a falsetto, the air and sound escapes through a small central portion of the folds that are squeezing together to enable a flute-like sound.

As kids we used to hold a blade of grass between our thumbs and blow through to make a high-pitched squeak. This, though not a totally accurate picture, will help give a sense of what's happening within the larynx.

When it's used in a lower pitch it loses volume and it becomes more obvious that it's a breathy sound without much power. (Think Marilyn Monroe singing, 'Happy Birthday, Mr President'.)

This tone is very useful when you feel yourself bumping up against the 'ceiling' of your chest voice – by retracting the false folds and lifting the soft palate, you can take away that jerky shift from head to chest voice. (Adolescent boys would love to be able to get a handle on this one to avoid those embarrassing squeaks that happen with the onset of puberty.)

> **TIP:** In Estill Training, the use of the terms 'head' and 'chest' voice is a no-no, the explanation being that our sound is produced by the vocal folds, not the head or the chest. While this is anatomically true, I've gone back to using these terms in working with people who don't know the technical explanation because it's an easy way for them to make sense of where they place the sound.

SPEECH

If you're male, you're probably using this singing quality already. You can replicate this sound by making an 'Oh-oh!' sound, meaning, 'Here comes trouble!'

Prolong this into long notes and you'll be in speech quality. That 'Oh-oh!' is also a handy way of adding a note or two to the lower part of your range, for which you'll naturally need a lowered larynx – otherwise you tend to lead into falsetto.

I've often found that women who come for sessions may

tend to hang around in a breathy falsetto, which works fine for high notes, but as soon as the pitch drops the power goes because the sound is breathy. This high falsetto tone works well when you're little, but sometimes women can stay at that stage, and their (singing) voice doesn't really progress to maturity.

Boys' voices break, forcing them to discover their speech quality. Boys in an all-male environment will tend to 'butch up' their voices as quickly as possible to avoid embarrassing squeaks, and gain a stronger position in the pack. Many women, however, shy away from bringing natural twang into their speech quality, feeling that it's too much or harsh or ugly. (This is sufficient when it comes to singing in a choir where this lack of power is masked by blending with the other voices in the line-up.)

Often when women come for sessions they identify that they want more power in their voice. They may express this as 'running out of breath', because they're stuck in falsetto that is breathy and expels all the air quickly. I love introducing these people to the authentic power of their voice. It's often found in a matter of minutes, and the results are dramatic. Sometimes people are surprised, and say, 'Is that my voice?'

CAN I LEARN PITCH?

I love to take on the challenge when people say to me, 'I can't sing.' I've convinced many people they're wrong when they say that. People will often use the expression, 'I'm tone deaf' (a rare condition), when what they're really saying is, 'I don't have a lot of experience in singing and I'm not confident.'

Over the years I've worked with several people who missed out on having pitch installed at an early age. We have a library of sounds stored within us and as each sound is received, we compare it with our database of sounds. When we sing, or speak, we measure the sounds we hear against our stored database, and in microseconds adjust by sending impulses to the multitude of muscles involved in making sound.

When we are little, our brains are like sponges, storing things like songs and remembering pitches quickly. As we get older the process slows down, but it is still possible to install pitch. I've had clients who had no singing at school or at home, and for them it often takes a lot of work to install. But for those who want to persist because, for instance, they want to join a choir, there is a pay-off. It may be a slow process, but the enjoyment that comes from mastering quite simple steps is worth it.

Those who are visual learners respond well to seeing the rise and fall of the notes marked on a whiteboard at a bit of a distance. (The distance factor helps with getting the voice out beyond a shy private biosphere, whereas singing to a page held in the hand tends to keep the sound held in close.)

I would recommend going to a singing teacher who teaches you to follow their voice, not notes on a piano. There's something harmonious about finding the blend in human voices, whereas an inability to match a piano could be quite alienating.

Many years ago, the first client I worked with who had this problem did her session in a room with a piano. I tried banging out the pitches and she randomly hit or missed, until after a while of this, I started to feel as if I couldn't match the piano either! Perhaps the human voice works better because there is a mutual desire to meet, and the initiator can almost pull the receiver toward them, at the same time making little micro adjustments in their own pitch to make a unified blend.

This remarkably complex pitching sequence can be cancelled when we sing along with music played into earphones, which dominates the feedback mechanism described above. The sound that comes out is notoriously off key!

In this instance, the listening function has been dominated, and can't act properly. Similarly, when I'm working with a choir and we need to tune up the accuracy of harmonies, the most obvious instruction is to sing at half volume. As the volume goes down, the listening goes up. In this case, people are not just hearing what goes on in their own head, rather, they become more aware of the sound of their neighbours.

CASE STUDY

Paula was an intelligent woman who'd had a host of learning problems at school. One of the ways it manifested was that she had difficulty identifying rhythm and pitch. We did some individual work to get her to the point where I would sound a note and she would lift her hand up and down, while sliding her note up or down, to find a match with mine. These sessions gave her the confidence to ask to join my choir, and when she did, she found that by singing softly next to someone confident, she could match pitches and find a unity that she felt she had missed so profoundly in her social interaction since childhood.

IN BRIEF

- Develop your understanding and control of The Three Throats.
- Develop your capacity for Twang, Sob, Falsetto, Vibrato and Speech qualities.

THE LONGING FOR COMMUNITY 8

Singing with other people is one of the most reliably joyful things we can do in this life. How often are you part of a group coming together in collaborative synergy, without competition? How often are you in a group where unity, mutual respect, cooperation, creative stimulation and joyful outcomes are the norm?

To quote psychologist Heather Gridley, who was one of the researchers in a survey conducted in 2011 by Victoria University:

> *Choirs provide structured community support and friendship – a natural antidote to feelings of isolation and loneliness ... Chanting and synchronising in harmony are ancient human rituals; they have sustained communities since time immemorial. The only difference now is that we have the science to prove it.*

I learned recently from a horse whisperer that horses can sense your heartbeat from 15 metres away. We humans can't tune into each other's heart rates so easily, and yet on some level we still know how to synchronise.

In 2013, Swedish musicologist Dr Björn Vickhoff conducted a study into the effect of music on our physiology and emotions.

Vickhoff used a group of fifteen high school choir members who were connected to pulse monitors and asked to sing a variety of material. Vickhoff and his team could see that as the choir sang in unison, their pulses began to match, speeding up and slowing down at the same time, and that this effect occurred very quickly across the group.

As we sing, we begin to control our breath in the same way as yogis do during their practice. The positive outcomes shared by both singing and yoga are a slowed down and less variable heart beat, which is associated with the relief of stress and anxiety, and is also helpful in reducing blood pressure.

Vickhoff explains:

'When you sing the phrases, it is a form of guided breathing. When you exhale, the heart slows down ... Our hypothesis is that song is a form of regular, controlled breathing, since exhaling occurs on the song phrases and inhaling between them.'

Indeed, when we sing together, we share and exchange the molecules in the air. We resonate in the same morphogenetic field; for a while we blend into unity and heal our feelings of separation.

Singing came before speech

The musical way in which we instinctively talk to infants (using a higher pitch than usual and long, drawn out vowels, with more descending pitch than normal speech), has been dubbed 'motherese' by researchers.

Babies respond very well to this type of speech, and research suggests that as well as singing and playing songs and lullabies to infants, 'motherese' helps them to acquire language. Some researchers working with evolutionary theory are wondering if this gave humans a survival advantage. It's also one of the demonstrations that first came singing, then came language.

Birds can sing to a few of their kin nearby, whales improvise on limited melodies but apparently don't sing in unison. Only humans can assemble as a horde and unite in song quite like this; no other species can unite in such large numbers.

For better or worse, national anthems have been known to cause an incredibly strong unifying effect for millions of people at a time – a surge of endorphins can generate a unique feeling of belonging and strong social bonding between people who make music together.

CASE STUDY

One of the Soulsong choir members, let's call her Phoebe, had been suffering from depression for years. She'd had a lonely and problematic childhood, which was probably caused by a compromised immune system.

She'd tried various anti-depressants, which were either ineffective or problematic. She'd tried alternative therapies, and counselling with varying degrees of success. A friend persuaded her to get through the door and into choir, and to her amazement, on the first night, for a while she totally forgot about her pain. That night she couldn't go to bed, let alone sleep, because her life energy that had been so stuck, was pouring out of her.

At the end of the first term, Phoebe came up to me and, slightly shyly, admitted to her past. The shame of it was fading partly because she was experiencing all the physiological shifts mentioned above, and partly because she had found herself embraced by the group in a way that she had no memory of in her childhood. My heart was gladdened to hear her say that while she still relied on counselling, 'This saves me a fortune in therapy!'

Want to feel better?

There is an excellent documentary, *The Musical Instinct: Science and Song*, which explores some of the latest research on this topic. It includes, for instance, a visual depiction of the increased blood flow in the brain after music lessons, and the thickening of the frontal cortex with prolonged musical training. It shows how music connects the auditory and motor systems; in other words, how music makes you just wanna get up and boogie. It demonstrates the stimulation of the brain's reward centre, the hypothalamus, increasing the dopamine flow in a way that, without music, we could probably only experience with drugs or sex.

> **TIP:** It's interesting to note that the word jazz comes from Creole French, *jazzer* – to make love.

The documentary also indicates how very young babies cry in relative pitches of thirds and fifths, while kids who are using a taunting 'NYAH NYAH' sound tend to use minor thirds.

It then moves onto the more universal level, exploring the notion that music is energy. Namely, the documentary states that, if string theory is correct, at the heart of matter is music. Each particle carries a vibrating 'string' and the mathematical equation that describes this is very similar to that of a vibrating string.

Moreover, Brian Greene, a physicist at Columbia University posits that the universe is a system of vibrating wave patterns. And here's one I really like: apparently black holes vibrate at B flat, a staggering 57 octaves below the waveband available to the human ear.

Ever since Einstein explained it to us a century ago, we've become less and less certain that the universe is solid, and more aware of the fact that our bodies are a mass of orbiting particles separated by vast amounts of space. Quantum physics has thrown more uncertainty and paradox into the mix, and many people have come to understand the notion that everything in the universe is made up of vibrations, or in other words, of sound and light.

It seems that every object has a natural set of frequencies at which it vibrates. When our voice makes harmonious sound, our whole body vibrates, and we influence the spin of the whirling particles into harmonious orbits. This is why, on a cellular level, singing makes us feel good. But enough of the quantum physics! Let's get back to a bit of anatomical certainty.

Long exhalations linked with vocalisation (as in chanting and singing) stimulate the vagus nerve, which connects the medulla oblongata to the striate nerves around the face, which are linked to the vagal regulation of the heart (one of the ways in which smiling affects your heart). It then passes through the carotid sheath down to the heart and the viscera.

This stimulation reduces tension in the face, the jaw and the neck. One of the results of this is that you actually look better! Until recently, this interaction was assumed to be a one-way relationship, as in the brain gives orders to the rest of the body. Advances in neuroscience now show this to be a two-way stream, and since we now know that we have as many neuropeptides and neurotransmitters in the gut as we do in the brain, then gut instinct has a basis in fact.

In short, the body's engagement in breath and vocalisation can drastically alter the way we think, feel and look.

OXYTOCIN

And finally, there is a strong connection between oxytocin and singing. Oxytocin is a string of nine amino acids released from the posterior pituitary, which developed as the mammalian brain evolved from the reptilian one. These amino acids flow throughout the whole brain reaching many parts of the nervous system.

Apart from being a 'reward' hormone, it also assists human cognition and plays a vital role in the strength of the immune system, allowing the body to adapt, protect and heal itself in the face of challenge. It reduces stress activity, and affects social behaviour by decreasing fear, making us more socially bold.

In addition, oxytocin increases trust, causing us to pay more attention to social stimuli, and activates our capacity for compassion. But wait, there's more! It's also an anti-inflammatory and anti-oxidant, which helps heal burns, cardiac problems, osteoporosis and mental disorders.

All of which points to one conclusion about the relationship between our body, our voice and our wellbeing. Wanna feel better? Get out there and sing!

In the last couple of decades there has been an upsurge in people learning singing in a group environment. You may be someone who has previously worked with a singing teacher, or maybe even only in the shower.

Non-professional singers may have the opportunity to get up and perform songs in front of an audience, maybe as a solo part in a choir performance, or with a band that's emerging from the garage, or some form of curated concert. This challenge has been known to strike terror in the bravest heart! Many would turn away at this point and say, 'Oh I could never do that.' If you can approach it with the right help, this challenge can be a wonderful, enriching and confidence-boosting experience. Tackling this challenge as a participant in a relatively small group is well worth it if you can find the right kind of singing teacher; one who knows how to help people over some of the obvious performance pitfalls, as well as tuning up their voice.

If a person simply gets up and sings their party piece, they could put on a show in a sort of anxious trance, but would perhaps sit down at the end and wonder what just happened. They would have very little memory of what they did between the beginning and the end of their song. The pressure of performance anxiety pushing adrenalin and cortisol through the system can create a syndrome known as 'leaving the body', as in leaving the present moment and going into a form of shock or trance.

Many big cities have at least one singing teacher who runs a group solo class where you can practise overcoming this form of stage fright. For many years now I've run one that I call Singing Solo, and I have strong opinions about how to help people overcome the above syndrome. If you're running or participating in a singing group, you might find useful tips in the following description of the process I use.

My process

First the group starts by acknowledging to each other the kind of fears that come up for them, noticing they're usually remarkably similar, which helps remove the alienated 'I'm the only one who ...' feeling. Each person also needs to state an intention for the work. This is the red thread that carries you through when things get challenging.

Next step is to practise breath and grounding techniques to deal with performance anxiety. There's a lot of detailed information about this in the chapters on Breath and Body Language.

Next the participant stands in front of the group and registers what it feels like to be observed, naming their feelings as they arise. For many people this evokes shameful, school experiences where they were put on the spot and somehow 'failed', so it's important to make them aware of this and show them that this is now a safe situation. (Make sure beforehand that this is true, and that you can trust the teacher to handle this situation or you may just re-enact old traumas. I have witnessed over and over how vulnerable a moment it can be to get up and sing to a group of people. If public speaking terrifies you, then singing may raise the stakes a whole lot higher. Many of the non-professional singers I've worked with have had an experience of someone hearing them singing and making a comment that they took very personally. It could have been a sibling, a parent, or the notorious music teacher who said, 'You stand up at the back and mime the words.' In many instances these people have perfectly adequate singing voices, but they've had years of believing otherwise. For a long time I blamed the notorious music teacher, but then I noticed that there were two very common phases when this would happen in people's lives; at age seven, or about seven years later in puberty. The seven-year cycle seems to hold special significance in human development and at these two times we can be hypersensitive to criticism. I like to help people to step beyond this to a place of freedom. The thoughts we had at age seven are no longer relevant to us as adults and they stand in the way, like the bars of a cage. These bars are mostly illusory and I love giving people the key to their cage.)

When people rehearse their solo, they may give off subtle signals that, on some level, they are reliving some form of early judgement. At this point it's important to guide a person back to presence, to enjoying, or at least appreciating, the sensation of 'This is me singing, this is me giving part of myself to you, this is me connecting to my essential being-alive-nowness.' One of the ways into this state is to get out of your own way and let the song come though. That sounds straightforward in theory but it's difficult to do in real life. A practical tip to help with that is to ask yourself 'What effect do I want this song to have on the listener?' This takes the focus off the singer, 'me', and puts it where it belongs.

Once the solo is finished I ask, 'Is there anything you'd like more or less of?' Notice this question is not about whether the singing is good or bad, which is the thing people want to talk about. This is merely about you stating intent and then doing something about it. It's important that you get more than one go at your song right away, that way you can explore your intention and the feedback in a practical way, and do something about modifying your singing. In some groups you may get one shot and then have to wait till next week, in which case you probably have to go over old ground to get back to the same place.

In a group setting a really important ingredient is being witnessed in tackling the challenge by the 'tribe'. The act of giving away and being witnessed by others apart from the teacher gives substance to the act, which could otherwise simply evaporate like a dream.

The final stage of this process involves checking with your stated fears from the beginning of the workshop, and noticing how a lot of the bars to the cage were past their use-by date. I'm not saying that they'll just vanish in a puff of smoke, but when they return you will have an antidote.

If you can be well guided through this challenge of singing

solo, you will probably have a breakthrough experience that has a flow-on effect to other corners of your life. Those bars of that cage that you installed when you were young were also inhibiting other ways that you express yourself, other ways in which, at an early age, you contracted, held back, went into hiding, in order to handle that shameful experience. When we are able to fully meet our fears head on, we move beyond them, and it often takes a challenging situation like this to bring them out from the dark corner they were hiding in, telling you to stay small. Some people get a similar effect from skydiving, but I would suggest that this is longer lasting and less risky or expensive.

SINGING SOLO

There is a beautiful nakedness in this act of singing solo because our voice, our persona, is so central to who we are. Many people feel they must carry around so many masks and so much armour to safely get through a day. After a while we forget that these are just survival strategies we've learned and perhaps needed when we were young and powerless, but they've now become so habitual that we think they're real. They can often be hiding a lurking, nagging thought that 'this is not really who I am and where I want to be', that 'real life is hopefully waiting for me somewhere in the future'.

The act of giving away our voice in song and being witnessed is a powerful way of stripping away the masks. When the witnesses applaud us for doing this, it's a powerful affirmation that we are whole and fine just as we are without our acquired identities, and that this is an essential, timeless part of being human. This essential place is where real life begins and it's never far away from us.

When I see people make this shift, I'm so touched by how radiant they look. That's the best word I can find to describe it. When people find this sweet spot in singing they literally look beautiful. At this moment, I'm convinced that what I see is someone in contact with their essential, divine self.

9 CHANTING AND MEDITATION

Rest in natural great peace
This exhausted mind
Beaten helplessly by karma
And neurotic thoughts
Like the relentless fury
Of the pounding waves
In the infinite ocean
Of samsara
Rest in natural great peace

Sogyal Rinpoche quoting his teacher,
Nyoshul Khenpo Jamming Dorji

According to the legend, the Chinese enlightened mystic Lao Tzu was visited by a monk who wanted to receive instruction on the path to enlightenment. The monk asked him what practices he should follow in order to attain the 'other shore'. Lao Tzu laughed and said, 'Other shore ... you're standing on it!'

Puzzled, the monk asked if he should pray more. Lao Tzu laughed again and said, 'Who are you talking to? There's nobody there!'

Seeing the monk's bewilderment, he took pity on him and gave him the following task, 'In order to attain the Holy Fruit, you must make pilgrimage to the Bridge of One Thousand Sighs, which joins this land to the other shore of the great Quan River, and there you must sing your prayers out loud.'

The monk did as he was bidden and made the arduous pilgrimage until finally he reached the fabled bridge, which, according to the legend, vibrated with musical tones when the wind blew from a favourable direction. Trembling to be so close to the end of his journey, he stepped up to the middle of the bridge and waited. After a while the monk thought, 'These tones are musical, but where is the answer to my question?'

Dutifully he started to chant his holy prayers, then suddenly, he noticed his feet vibrating with the music of the planks of the bridge, and then his thighs, and his belly and so on, up to his Third Eye. In an instant came a flash of satori, and he let out a call of joyous thanks all the way up to the skies.

For in an instant, he realised what Lao Tzu had tried to tell him when he said there is no other shore. He saw that the self and the other, the inner and the outer, became one, when the breath of his prayers vibrated as pure sound. His body became pure sound and thus he was pure and whole.

A modern version of prayer

For centuries, Buddhists and Sufis have treated chanting as the bridge between body, mind and spirit. The prolonged out-breaths involved slow down the heart rate, relax the mind and body, and downgrade our fight/flight responses, thus helping to reduce anxiety. Chanting can still the mind-chatter from pounding waves to a still lake. When we close our eyes and chant, we have the chance to cease being a body and become pure sound, which can give us easy access to soothing the exhausted mind, and recapturing that longed for sense of unity.

In Christian mythology, this is portrayed as getting back to the Garden of Eden, and in heaven there seems to be not much else to do but strum harps and sing. Hindus and Buddhists aim for Nirvana, enlightenment, the flowering of the thousand-petalled lotus. In atheist terms, it might be explained as a subconscious memory, a longing to return to the warm, free, floating state in the womb.

Professor Sarah Wilson from the Melbourne University School of Psychology describes chanting and synchronising in harmony as 'ancient rituals, they have sustained communities since time immemorial, the difference now is that we have the science to prove it.'

It is said that the Christian mystic St Francis of Assisi died singing prayers of praise and glory. For a long time I assumed prayer was a rather childish activity that involved sending a form of shopping list to some father figure asking for a bit of special attention. Then, years ago, a spiritual teacher whispered in my ear a single word to explain the true meaning of prayer: Gratitude.

The spiritual teacher Osho said that the modern Western mind was far too busy and electrified to be able to drop into the simplicity of the traditional vipassana meditation practice (of witnessing the breath and the thoughts) without some sort of prior discharging of all that busyness. He devised active meditations designed to do just that, and my time at the ashram in Pune, in India, and at the Humaniversity in Amsterdam, gave me the wonderful experience of long bouts of respite from 'the exhausted mind'.

I'd had a bit of (self-conscious) experience of trying to chant in Sanskrit, but this stirred up 'more relentless fury of the pounding waves'. This all changed when, years ago, the simplicity of Osho's Nadhabrahma meditation revealed to me how to drop deep within through chanting.

For a demonstration of this, search YouTube for the Osho Nadhabrahma Meditation, and for an excellent explanation of the need for active meditations, search on Osho: the need for dynamic meditation.

> **TIP:** Osho speaks very slowly in order for your mind to slow down while listening.

In the chapter Breath: Our Constant Companion, we saw how manipulation of the breath can create mood states – from fear, to pain, to anger and love. Try this exercise and see for yourself how the long exhalations of chanting work.

Exercise: Critical or compassionate?

- When we take a long, steady in-breath, we look at the world more critically.
- When we take a long, steady out-breath, we look at the world more compassionately. (Enhance this by opening the palms in a gesture of giving and receiving.)

Discontent and re-membering

The word religion comes from the Latin *ligare*, to bind, therefore *re-ligare* means to bind back. Allegedly, the last word the Buddha spoke was 'sammasati', which translates as 'right remembering'. There are some theologians who say the word repent in the Bible has lost its original sense of 'returning', 'coming back' or 're-membering', and is not necessarily linked to sin, but instead, to that very human capacity to lose track of what's good for us. Buddhism takes a more compassionate view of 'straying from the path of righteousness' than Christianity traditionally has, and 'right remembering' is an act of reunification of a dis-membered self.

Quantum physics tells us that the world only appears to be solid, and that between the orbiting atoms that bind us together, there are vast amounts of space. Even the atoms, which appear to be solid, on examination dissolve into pure vibration of sound and light. Chanting and singing help to re-member these wavelengths, arranging the mass of whirling particles that make up our human body into harmonic orbits. At the same time it raises our oxytocin levels, lowering our cortisol and blood pressure ... no wonder it feels good!

I've seen anecdotal evidence of this in my weekly Soulsong choir that has been running now for over ten years. People say things like:

- 'I feel like I've just had a massage.'
- 'Because I have toddlers, I don't have time in my day to meditate, so this is my once-a-week meditation practice.'

Or in the lunchtime choir that I ran in a large hospital:

- 'This really shifts my energy and helps me get through the afternoon.'

In the last three decades, gospel choirs have become immensely popular, tuning into the sacred songs that gave African Americans the spiritual uplift to help them through years of slavery, as well as accompanying their ongoing struggle for justice in the present day. In gospel choirs, many atheists find joy in singing about Jesus and heaven. As Kiwi gospel choir-leader extraordinaire Tony Backhouse once put it, 'It's hard to sing "Baby, baby" after you've sung, "Lord! Lord!"'

Singing: prayer or meditation?

In the West, the ancient Christian notion of prayer has perhaps been superseded by meditation (in terms of the number of people actually practising it).

Ideally, meditation creates a 180-degree shift from looking for God out there (somewhere else), instead turning inwards to a deeper dimension of self, until ultimately that self (the small ego-bound me), dissolves. The wave realises that it does not have to struggle to maintain itself as separate from the ocean, and dissolves to become part of the whole again. It re-members its true nature.

The rise and fall of in-breath and out-breath that sustains long-held notes or chants has the capacity to form a bridge between the inner and outer world. I've heard it said that prayer is talking to God, and meditation is listening to God.

In Sufi and early Gnostic traditions, it was a great secret and privilege to be initiated into the (usually men-only) group who were allowed to chant the names of God. To utter the name of God without being initiated was to expect a good deal of smiting for such a profane act.

The men would gather, preferably in a stone building for its acoustic properties, and chant for hours, getting very tranced out, for instance riffing on the name of the God of Judea, 'Yahweh'. He is the taproot of our modern-day version of God, the one who in the Old Testament said, 'I thy God am a jealous God. Thou shalt have no other gods but me.' In other words, 'take my name in vain and expect to be smitten!' Logically therefore, only the chosen could have access to this meeting with God.

Imagine a group of singers sitting in a circle in an acoustically sympathetic room, chanting a long single note. If they keep going, after a while their heart rate and brainwaves align – entrainment. Slowly the combination of harmonic overtones in all the voices creates separate higher notes that ring out so strongly it seems as if someone overhead is singing, an impossibly high tone. If you've ever sat in such a circle, you can see how the ancients felt they were visited by the voices of the angels ... and who's to say they weren't?

10 VOICE: AN AID TO CURING SOCIETY'S ILLS

This chapter looks at voice as a unifying force for community. It looks at ways that voice can heal society's aches and pains. Let's start by contemplating the following questions. How often are you part of a group coming together in collaborative synergy, without competition? How often are you in a group where mutual respect, cooperation, creative stimulation, and joyful outcomes are the norm?

How the Beatles became bigger than Jesus

A few years ago, when I was on the board of Community Music Victoria, a group of us was contracted to run singing workshops at Port Fairy Folk Festival. Bernard Carney, a singer-songwriter from Perth was leading a band that was going to do Beatles songs in the bar the next night, and knowing that I was born near Liverpool, he asked me if I wanted to join in for some of the songs.

It was appealing, so I went along to the bar to check out the venue. It was a huge combination of two marquees joined together, big enough to hold about a thousand people. A quintet was playing Celtic tunes and standing at the back, I could faintly hear the band singing over the din of the bar. (Performing to an alcohol-laden audience is horrible. Standing on stage you can feel this chaotic wall of noise coming at you. Don't expect to be heard!)

I left the bar, vowing that hell would freeze over before I'd get up there. Next night, I went along to show support, and noticed that within fifteen minutes, the front few rows were joining in with the Beatles songs. Within an hour, the whole place was singing. I was standing next to a group that seemed like university students, and I asked them 'How come you know this stuff?' To which one of them replied, 'Well, our parents played this to us in our cots. You'd do the same for your kids, wouldn't you?'

So there was a crowd of three generations of people, who all knew most of the words to these songs. A couple of hours later, when I left, the crowd was still singing.

Voice as a unifying force

The sixties came along with a big clear-out of the old, but it seems that in this regard, a few cultural babies were thrown out with the bath water. The traditional hymns began to fade with the old people. Now we have Beatles songs in common. (And I love almost every one of 'em!)

Yes, if you know where to look you'll clearly hear the Beatles, English and Irish folk roots (Liverpool was the first stopping-off port from Eire). But in the collision between rock and folk music, it was rock that won. When jive and the jitterbug dropped out of fashion, partner dancing came to an end. (A tragedy, perhaps?) Now we dance separately in a crowd, and while there is also a wonderful, tribal, elemental ingredient to this, you can feel very much alone.

Before the Industrial Revolution, work songs were common. They made the day pass quicker and brought people together to work in a similar rhythm. Sea shanties are an example of getting a team of men to all haul in the same rhythm. The Lomax Brothers made some excellent field recordings of chain gang songs in Alabama prison farms in the late thirties. You can hear a gang of African-American convicts singing in two- and three-part harmony while swinging picks for twelve hours in the hot sun. The quality of their singing is magnificent, despite the double call on their oxygen in singing and hammering at the same time. With the arrival of factories and the noise of machinery, work songs became inaudible above the din, becoming more and more irrelevant. Each worker became more isolated and more alienated from their work.

In post-war Western culture, when summer brought people out into the park, a new recreation started. The under-forties listened to that new invention, the transistor radio, which meant one thing: portable music. They could pick it up, take it out of the living room, away from 'the olds', and would gather in pairs and groups to listen to Top of the Pops all at the same time across the country. Come Monday morning, at work or school, most of them knew what was number one and it was quite normal to sing bits of it together.

Now everyone can have whatever music, whenever, on their private, separate headset and the most common publicly shared listening music is the stuff they're piping around you at the supermarket.

Joseph Campbell once said if you want to see what a society values most, look to its biggest buildings. Here in Melbourne, I live near Chadstone – what may be the biggest shopping centre in the Southern Hemisphere. Every Sunday the car park is full, with lines of traffic queuing to get in, consumers hungry to buy what will soon become Chinese-made landfill.

Those who travel past this shopping centre may notice that there's a gigantic sculpture out the front of the main entrance, a vast conglomeration of shapes wrought out of unprimed steel that's intentionally allowed to turn a rusty brown. However, few people notice that as you approach the sculpture heading west into the city, the interlocking forms assemble themselves into the shape of a heart. Drive a little further and they rearrange themselves into a dollar sign. Whether this is intentional or not, it always provokes me to consider the larger picture of our society's priorities.

The commercialisation of music has spawned an industry that wants us to consume as much merchandise as possible, and for years has tried to hype us into believing that this next band will be 'bigger than the Beatles'. Don't get me wrong, this is not some conservative rant about going back to the glory days, it's more of a call to stop and check in where you want to position yourself in society.

Music is not just a consumption medium, it's as perennial as the grass, and still alive and well in the upsurge of young people who really want to make a career out of creating and playing music. As mentioned, Community Music Victoria has 850 choirs on its books, and this does not include the many who are singing in choirs or garage bands or informal jams all around the rest of the country.

Community and communion

Singing in a choir offers the possibility of creating rather than consuming music, while at the same time creating community. It can transform the metaphor of harmony into a lived experience. Moreover, it can be a tangible manifestation of the power and joy of cooperation and a way of making music with very little specialist training.

Voice is a musical instrument that most people have easy access to, and playing that instrument can inspire transformative, uplifting experiences that dispel pain and heal differences.

How often do you physically experience harmony? Do you play an instrument in a creative, collaborative way? How often do you explore a creative art form that's collaborative?

Songs carry our culture – society's collective stories, memories and dreams. When the English wanted to dominate the Scots and the Irish, they took away their musical instruments. There was a time when it was illegal for an Irishman to own an instrument, but the spirit of music is irrepressible in Ireland, so they devised a form of mouth music and would dance to that. One surviving piece of mouth music has a verse that says, 'Dance to your shadow when it's good to be living lad. Dance to your shadow when there's nothing better near.'

I love that sense of a joyful, musical spirit, so alive it wants to dance to its own shadow. This relationship with music honours a spirit that moves through us, and becomes a co-creation of common culture.

Voice as a way of healing

One of the reasons I wrote this book is that, again and again in sessions, I'm attempting to get people to give themselves permission to sing and speak out loud. Sometimes it's downright painful to see glimpses of people's past, as they bump into the bars of that cage they built for themselves in order to survive earlier in life.

The act of making a large, clear sound is something that the body, and our whole being craves. If you haven't sung or yelled out loud recently, then there's a major part of you that's been neglected, and maybe even stuck inside. Current psychological theory suggests that anger that is consistently blocked from being released can lead to depression. The energy that it takes to hold back and deny it sucks our life force away.

Unfortunately, now that singing is not a mandatory part of the school curriculum, many kids are missing out on this important part of their self-expression. They don't get to hear their voice ring out in the classroom in a way that is separate from the pressure of right/wrong answers. If you get to yell on the sports field, then great!

And what of all the other nuances that singing brings? I know when I was going through my own teenage 'You don't understand!' phase, I'd sit on my bedroom window ledge and sing mournful Dylan songs over the rooftops. I reckon it saved my life.

Singing stimulates the vagus nerve

This nerve system is the second biggest after the spinal nerve system, and extends all the way down from the medulla oblongata through the striate muscles of the face – which connect a smile with your heart – through the neck, alongside the carotid artery, directly to the heart, and then on down to the viscera. We often think of the brain as being the control room, sending messages out to the body, but in fact, the belly and the heart are constantly sending messages to the brain, via the vagus nerve. This nerve system responds to the long exhalations of the breath and the vibration of singing, especially the effect of singing on the striate muscles of the face.

There is an excellent online tutorial by Peter Levine PhD entitled Sexual Trauma: Healing the Sacred Wound. In it he demonstrates how stimulating the vagus nerve through intoning the sound 'Vu', down through the viscera to the pelvic floor can help heal the kind of sexual traumas that some of us have experienced or inherited.

Singing as a shame-buster

A while ago I started volunteering in the Royal Melbourne Hospital Eating Disorders Unit, getting people singing. During the earlier sessions, you could cut the atmosphere with a knife. The scene looked like this: nine outpatients and a resident psychologist in a small room where each chair had a cushion on it. As soon as they sat down, the cushion would go on their lap. The silence was awkward; everyone mostly looked at their shoes.

There was a clunky little CD player on the table, and I put on a soundtrack that played a form of ambient music that guided the listener to sing notes going up through an octave and back down again, over the course of fifteen minutes. The first time I played it there was hardly any vocal sound, and when we'd finished I asked for feedback and consistently heard, 'relaxing'.

A common factor of an eating disorder is a high state of anxiety, and a strong need for control. Many of the participants were students with very high school marks and an unfortunate tendency to perfectionism. Anything that helps relaxation has to be a bonus.

One week I forgot to bring the CD and we did it unaccompanied. The following week I was pleasantly surprised: the patients asked to stick to this a cappella method. They were getting bolder, and we started singing songs that had harmonies.

We often do an exercise where everyone stands, looks out of the window and imagines hailing a taxi with a loud 'HEEEEY!' It's a wonderful loud cacophony, and a great antidote to keeping quiet until you've got it perfectly right.

My Thursday mornings at the hospital touch me deeply. I'm struck by the fragility in the room, and at the same time the courage of those who dare to make it through the door and let themselves be seen and heard.

One Thursday morning I was feeling a bit rough, and as I walked past the emergency unit, past the smokers with broken bodies in wheelchair, I had to steel myself a little to go through the main entrance; I would rather have been on the train back home.

I realised that if this act was hard for me, it was much harder for those who were coming back this morning to the place where recently they had been an inpatient. If you find yourself on the inpatient ward at an eating disorder unit, you know you've reached a dangerously low point in your life. It is, in fact, the mental disorder with the highest death rate.

At the end of that Thursday session I acknowledged the courage it must have taken to get through the door that morning, and mentioned that it pointed out a life metaphor: sometimes we just have to 'get through the door'. We may duck and swerve and procrastinate, but sometimes we just have to really show up, so that life can lift us up onto its shoulder.

After ten weeks of morning singing sessions the group became downright rowdy, yelling out, cracking jokes and proffering feedback words like 'freer', 'more confident', louder', and 'open'. I've always known that voice work can be a healing modality, but I could never have imagined such a rapid and dramatic shift.

The act of vocalising, clear and strong, is deeply cleansing and uplifting. The belly muscles squeeze the diaphragm so that the lungs may push air through the vocal folds. Many of the muscles of the outer sheath of the torso are similarly engaged, and at the same time it vibrates the body from the inside – it's a great form of massage!

The action of the belly muscles squeezing is a smaller, gentler version of the action we use when we vomit and when we sob. With the latter two, the body is working to expel something from inside us that it registers as toxic, or something to be released. Singing is a much gentler form of releasing emotion, be it sad or joyous.

Singing up Country

In ancient cultures, such as that of Aboriginal Australia, or the Celtic and Sufi traditions, knowledge was not stored and handed down in writing. The way of passing on stories that carried vital information such as the maps of the country, or the learned wisdom of generations, was by singing them. The melody carried the information into the memory and helped it to stick.

Aboriginal groups could travel vast stretches of this continent without maps, as long as they knew the songlines. They would 'sing up Country' in a way that remains largely mysterious to our post-Enlightenment minds. Unfortunately, that singing is now severely restricted by an overlay of concrete and deep mining trenches, but it's not entirely forgotten.

In her award-winning documentary *Putuparri and the Rainmakers*, Nicole Ma shows elders travelling on a healing journey, back to their country in the Western Desert, which they had to leave in their youth. They travel for days, following some inbuilt navigation into an almost inaccessible piece of land. In the middle of this desert they track down what looks like a small puddle. They start to call and dance and sing to the totem spirits of the place, and before long a huge, drought-breaking thunderstorm appears in the middle of this desert, and once again, their sacred spot becomes a lake.

Releasing toxicity

I once saw some documentary footage of an Amazonian Indian speaking in his language about how angry he was that ranchers were moving in and mowing down his tribal home, the rainforest, to make way for beef cattle. What he said was interspersed with lots of spitting, blowing sounds, and at first I thought it was something to do with the weapon of choice around there being blow-darts. Then I realised that, in talking about his enemies, he was also blowing them away. It has been said that we must choose our enemies wisely for we will eventually become like them, if only by pushing hard on a dichotomy of opposites. What the Amazonian was doing was strongly engaging his belly muscles to blow away, and to expel the enemy from inside him. In that sense, his voice and his body were very wise.

11 VOICE AND THE SHADOW

Bad guys get the best parts.

When Carl Gustav Jung introduced the notion of the shadow self to western psychology, he described something that actors had known for centuries. Briefly put, he was referring to all the socially unacceptable parts of ourselves that early in life we throw down into the basement of the subconscious. We do this in order to survive.

Our custodians, the people bigger than us, make it clear (with some mixed messages), what is acceptable behaviour from us in order for us to function in the world as we know it. Most of us have learned that yelling and screaming like a two-year-old doesn't cut it, however, we still have the basic, primal impulses of our reptilian brain.

As we become more civilised, our frontal cortex develops impulse control, and we rarely notice that it's actually making most of our impulses all but invisible unless some extreme situation unleashes them. As an example, soldiers in battle (from what we hear from those who dare to talk about it afterwards), are driven to a kind of madness that gives ordinary people the power to commit extreme heroism, or atrocities in a chaotic kill-or-be-killed situation.

Exploring this shadow side goes hand in hand with voice work. Since contemporary theatre demands more than just actors speaking words, if you're working on your voice, you'll need to find out what emotional extremes it's capable of. Actors are expected to be physically adept, and it's disturbing to see someone using techniques of physical theatre with a voice that can't keep up.

My first understanding of working with the shadow came after I'd finished theatre school, when I was in a week-long workshop with Sigmund Molyk, the actor and voice specialist in the laboratorium of the Polish theatre director Jerzy Grotowski. As a director, Grotowski was hugely influential on Western theatre from the late sixties onwards, and many people made the pilgrimage to Wrocław to study with him.

I say pilgrimage, because the Iron Curtain was drawn definitely shut at the time and getting into Poland was no easy feat. What's more, Grotowski's training was famous for being physically, mentally and spiritually exhausting. Those who came back brought with them a new way of working, one that helped break the prevailing tradition of theatre as a literary medium where the author reigned supreme and his (mostly male) will was interpreted by the demi-god: the director.

Prior to Grotowski, actors were mainly a vehicle for words written by someone else, and their job was to be a (relatively) pure vessel for the text. Grotowski's notion of a Poor Theatre was revolutionary at the time, and the book *Towards a Poor Theatre* was for decades to come a bible in progressive circles at theatre schools. Grotowski asked his actors to embody characters, often in a visceral, physically demanding way, rather than relying on just text to convey meaning. This tended to convey the animal nature of the human condition lying beneath the veneer of civilisation.

Sigmund Molyk went to work on me in that workshop, where I had just presented my showpiece: Macheath's final speech and song from *Threepenny Opera*. I thought I'd done quite a polished job on it, until Molyk said in a thick Polish accent, 'You are going to breeng the deveel up out of the ground!'

Back then I had only a hint of a clue what he meant. He was about to expand my voice by getting me to commit to an extremely physical avenue of approach. It was as if I had to twist and turn myself inside out to take myself to the level of intensity required to embody the archetype of the devil.

There followed an hour of howling, grunting and sweating, turning myself inside out in front of my fellow participants. When I look back, I'm eternally grateful to him for introducing me to my shadow. We've all got one or two lurking inside us. Perhaps the most common way people experience this is road rage, but remember, when just for a few seconds your 'killer' reared its head and snarled at a total stranger? If you heard a recording of your voice at that moment (scary thought), you'd probably be listening to the outer limits of the emotional intensity you can pack into your voice.

That day Sigmund Molyk taught me something I've often used since in coaching sessions, in a much gentler form. One of the quickest ways to bring about a change in vocal quality is to start with some change in body posture or attitude. The voice responds so much better to this than an intellectual approach.

12 VOICE SECRETS FROM THE ACTING PROFESSION

This chapter will introduce you to some of the lesser-known avenues of voice work that actors may discover in their training, and show how exploring this kind of work can reap enormous benefits for the layperson. If you have the opportunity to do this work, it will be a great help in uncovering your authentic voice.

It's good for your voice

There are three basic fears people have of their voice:

- It's not big enough.
- It's not interesting enough.
- It's too much (or in other words, fear of totally letting go of self-consciousness, which is in the same family as fear of orgasm. Oh yes – some people find that scary).

Now that last comment may seem like an extravagant claim, but if we consider how many forums there are for normal adults in

Western society to express extreme pleasure, the ones that come to mind are sporting events, choirs and non-classical concerts.

Notice how often at a musical gig where people are yelling appreciation, a lot of males will soften their tone by going up into a yell in their higher, falsetto register. Those who don't might come out with a kind of yell like a haka, the Maori battle cry, and how many men at that gig want to feel like they're starting a war?

Even the most indulgent parents need to teach kids the difference between their inside and outside voices, and of course there are so many more of society's pressures between then and adulthood that weigh in whenever we think we've expressed ourselves too freely, and the resulting shame that closes in is strongly formative. How often in working with helping people expand their voice have I seen that universal gesture of withdrawal: a hand that quickly goes up the mouth to try and push back the words or sound that just came out.

ACTING IS THE SHY PERSON'S REVENGE

For eleven years I co-devised and facilitated a workshop called Acting, Playing and Being with Alka (Penelope Chater). Between us we had decades of experience as leading acting teachers, and also in meditation and personal development. We consistently enjoyed teaching the basics of acting training to people who had little or no experience of it, and the delight was in helping people take those first hugely incremental steps into expansiveness and freedom. We did a lot of cross-germination between personal development exercises and acting exercises, and the beauty of it was that people could enter into a dyad where, for instance, they acted out two people having a shouting argument, without the messy consequences that usually accompanied that act.

We'd give the two participants a script or a simple framework for improvising, and before long they'd be at it like an old married couple who'd honed their particular sticking point with years of practice. Most people found that this work was great fun, and incidentally it was also therapeutic, except, unlike an actual argument, there was very little personal investment required, nor any consequences beyond a tremendous feeling of expansiveness. Many participants found that it was the first time in years that they'd been in a shouting match with another human being, and consequently, the exercise would leave them with a hoarse voice. Most kids can shout all day. Adults sometimes need to re-learn this. Later in this chapter is a description of the preparation needed to re-learn how to shout without strain.

Exercise: Widen your waveband

Most people learned early in life to put invisible barriers around themselves and stick to a narrow waveband of normal behaviour for fear of ostracism, public humiliation, or being locked up. There's a wonderful expansiveness that comes from exploring simple techniques that help people hop over these barriers and explore a larger life.

Here's a warm-up exercise, borrowed from a centuries old improvisation technique called *commedia dell'arte*. This was an obvious precursor to the above-mentioned argument exercise.

- Participants are asked to imagine they are two characters standing at opposite ends of a narrow bridge, gradually approaching each other. The bridge is so narrow that when they meet, they will have to swivel closely around each other. It may take as long as two minutes to cross the bridge. All the while, one character is laughing as loud and manically as possible at the other, while character number two is crying, howling with the shame of being so humiliated. Often a deep realisation comes when, at the midpoint of their swivel, they swap roles and the laugher is now humiliated. These two emotions are not at odds with each other, they're just flip sides of the coin of human experience.
- These roles can be varied as an, 'I love you/you stink' swap or 'I need you/I'm indifferent'. Mostly this exercise generates an incredible amount of noise, and the interesting thing about the laugh/cry version is that people notice this enlarged effort of emotional extremes uses the same belly muscles for both ends of the spectrum and generally leaves them aching with the effort.

- A large voice requires strong effort, particularly from the muscles of the lower belly. In fact, so many of the muscles of the torso, and even the thighs, are engaged in producing an enlarged sound. Singing and yelling are full body experiences.

CASE STUDY

When we chose a part for our participants to play in the final performance, we often cast them against type, that is, we chose something that at first sight was the opposite of their natural characteristics, mainly for its liberating effect.

Jonathan was a shy academic who literally stumbled into his first class. His love life seemed to be a collection of tales of unrequited love. We facilitated his growing into the role of Mike from Steven Berkoff's East. *This is play that combines a high-flown (mock) classical language, with the cockney slang of London's East End, in the mouths of characters who are rough, tough, live-for-the-moment people. It's also a form of theatre that is very embodied, reflecting Berkoff's training in mime and other forms of physical theatre.*

Jonathan worked on a monologue in which Mike is bragging to a prospective female conquest about the wonderful qualities of his penis, in a loud cockney voice with much gesturing and acting out. This was a bit of a challenge for Jonathan, but he managed it, much to the amazement of his friends who came to see him in performance.

Exercise: Emotional directors

Jonathan had grown attached to a certain comfortable way of being, and liked his emotions and his response to them as predictable as possible. Of course, before we sit in judgement of Jonathan, we have to acknowledge that something similar applies to most of us too. This exercise helps participants loosen some of that attachment.

- Two people are given a simple scene to act out, e.g. a pick-up in a bar, or a visit to a customer service counter. Their objectives are simple, and without the following intervention, two inexperienced performers would probably come up with something clunky and clichéd. Each of these participants is assigned a director who has flash cards with large letters on them with verbs such as criticise, seduce, flatter, etc. Pretty soon the directors work out how to heat their actors up, and have them leaping to wild extremes of emotion; the absurdity of it often has the audience in stitches. Because the scene is ridiculously overheated and messy, participants find themselves diving into extreme standpoints before their censorship filters can intervene. Emotions are, by their nature, often messy. From here it's a shorter step to allowing more emotional colour.

Clients who come for voice work often say they think their voice is monotone, and they'd like more colour. Obviously the above exercise is part of committed group training and outside of the domain of an individual session, however, an equivalent piece of work would be to give the client an expressive piece of text, speaking as a character very different from their everyday self.

Exercise: Declarations of love

Here's one of my favourite pieces and a great way to make contact with the colour of your voice. The Duke Orsino in *Twelfth Night* is driven to distraction with unrequited love. His extravagant declarations swing between joy and frustration as he wants and wants and wants, while his court musicians attempt to satisfy his whims. It's a good starting point because there's very little abstraction, he's very passionate, and he's very much in the here and now. It doesn't have to be gender specific and easily transfers to the desires of a duchess.

> **Twelfth Night (Act 1, Scene 1)**
> If music be the food of love, play on;
> Give me excess of it, that surfeiting
> The appetite may sicken and so die –
> That strain again; It had a dying fall:
> Oh! It came o'er my ear like the sweet sound
> That breathes upon a bank of violets

Stealing and giving perfume. Enough! No more;
'Tis not so sweet now as it was before.
Oh spirit of love how quick and fresh art thou!

- Sing this passage extravagantly.
- Speak it as you would to establish a rapport with someone significant to you.
- If you fear running out of breath, sing/chant each continuous line of thought or action.
- Remove the consonants and speak just the vowels. Strange though this may seem, it frees up the music of the text and connects speaking to the whole body.
- Come back to speaking the text fully. Notice you're more able to fully inhabit the piece now.

TIP: For those who don't already know, the text above has an underlying rhythm of iambic pentameter, where each line moves to a beat of five. (This comes from the Greek for foot – *iamb* – and five – *penta*.) Greek choruses danced as they chanted the narrative, the most common rhythm of their feet similar to a heart beat, DE DUM, DE DUM, DE DUM … So you'll notice that Shakespeare stresses and softens alternate syllables. The underlying rhythm brings out a heightened value to the text that in modern times we'd associate with singing.

CASE STUDY

Imogen was a tall, charismatic executive who was accustomed to a place of fairly high status within a law firm. She was also used to keeping things polite, and a little formal. She'd gone straight from school to college to a career path through a couple of mid-tier law firms and had absorbed the ethos of the industry without having much experience in a working life outside that world. We gave her the part of Martha from Who's Afraid of Virginia Woolf?

Martha drinks a lot, and she flirts with, or seduces, younger men when she can. She is, in her own words, 'loud and vulgar', and says 'I wear the pants in this house because somebody has to!'

We could see that Imogen needed something to help her break through years of habitual politeness. The following exercise, Rediscovering the Warrior, was a breakthrough for her and afterwards, in rehearsal she loved to stumble round, glass in hand, trashing anyone within earshot.

Exercise: Rediscovering the Warrior

This exercise would come later in the training than the *commedia dell'arte* exercise mentioned earlier, which is easily accessible and usually ends in laughter. It's not for the faint-hearted and often involves careful side-coaching.

- Each participant would stand facing a line-up of at least six people who stood facing them, each one about two metres behind the other, as 'obstacles' to overcome. The participant was then required to work their way down the line, removing the obstacles by saying, 'Get out of my way.' The task of the obstacles was to move away only when they were convinced that this person really meant it – when they had contacted their archetypal warrior-self, and transcended the normal checks and balances that hide our full capacity. People often discover they can tap into an incredible source of power lying dormant within. Understandably, this exercise needs careful handling and debriefing afterwards.

CASE STUDY

Of course, having a charismatically powerful voice does not have to entail being loud. The above exercise was an essential step for Brian, who was given the part of the devil, a piece of script from the film The Devil's Advocate, *as played by Al Pacino.*

Brian was a therapist who cared for his clients, and would in no way want to manipulate or damage them. It was therefore an unusual stretch for him to play such a character, and yet for this part he needed a definite gravitas to persuade his listeners.

Now, the devil is a pretty hefty archetype to embody, and not an easy one to pull off without making a joke of it, or seeming like a melodramatic villain. Again, his friends in the audience were amazed to see this side of Brian, and far from being repelled, found themselves quite enthralled by him.

Shouting

I once had to play a sergeant major-type character yelling at all the other actors on stage, non-stop, for the first fifteen minutes of a two-hour performance, which ended in ten of us running to the front of the stage and singing a four-part harmony. I was responsible for giving the starting note, and I had a very narrow margin for error. If I got it wrong, I would definitely hear from either the top or bottom section back in the dressing room.

When we first did a week-long run of this show, I learned the hard way how not to shout! I was straining too hard with the top half of my body, while pushing air and energy hard from down below. The result was a classic split between the top and bottom halves of my body. As a result, two nights into the run I was struggling to make sound, let alone pitch a four-part harmony at the end of the show. Very scary!

> **TIP:** Did you know that if you shout properly for an extended period, you'll feel your thigh muscles engage and even shake as they help you ground all that energy?

If you've followed the warm-ups in the chapter All You Need to Get Started, you'll have cleared the way. As mentioned, shouting needs to come from way down in the thighs. The section from your lips to your collarbone needs to be open and free.

Exercise: Shouting without strain

- Take a strong, grounded stance.
- With the back of the neck long, create a long resonant 'tube' from your knees to the crown of the head.
- Reach your hands forward as if to lift something heavy.
- Call, 'Woe!' long and clear, feeling as if you're pulling this sound up and out of the ground.
- Extend the call longer, possibly louder, checking all the while that there's no resistance/tickling/rasping in the throat, and no build-up of pressure in the head.
- Try a long 'No!' sound, or if that is still tricky, just a long 'Ho!'
- Point as you try these lines, written for the character of Lady Anne to hurl at Richard III, who has just murdered her husband.
  'Blush! Blush! Though lump of foul deformity!'
  'Out of my sight!'
  'Thou dost infect mine eyes!'
- Notice all those wonderful plosive and spitting sounds that Shakespeare gives you to complete the effect.
- Start slowly, focusing on vowels and de-emphasising the consonants. As you pick up speed to make it more of a naturalistic tempo, check that your throat is open and free, your neck is long and there's no rasping that indicates that chaotic escape of air that bangs the vocal folds together.

'Yes and ...'

I've done a lot of work with lawyers and barristers, who operate in an adversarial profession. Often, their job is to find the 'Yes, but ...' to pick holes in another's story, to find something wrong. After a few years, this can become a fixed stance in the world, and the legal profession is waking up to the fact that this is a major contributor to the high rate of depression among lawyers.

I learned the following exercise early in my training as an actor, and have consistently used it ever since whenever I'm about to embark on a creative project with people. At first the exercise needs a side coach because as adults we can very easily slip back into a 'Yes, but ...' However, it's soon easy to pick up and it serves as an antidote to blocked thought processes by giving the mind free rein, and seeing just what it's capable of when you give the Judge, the Critic and the Censor the slip.

Exercise: 'Yes, and ...'

- Two people are given a topic to discuss, fast and enthusiastically. (It's best to start with an absurd topic so that everyone is automatically an expert, e.g. 'The day I landed on Mars.')
- Person A talks at speed.
- As soon as person A goes blank, person B takes over, always beginning with the two words, 'Yes, and ...' so that each

- person is supporting the other rather than debating the other.
- The rules are simple; no questions, just statements. (You can't answer a question with 'Yes, and ...) No interruptions (that's a 'Yes, but ...') Listen carefully, stay in the moment so that you can always pick up where the other left off, not where they were five seconds ago, but now. Clearly, as well as being about creative flow, it's also about the art of listening and staying in the present with someone.

I remember one night in Sydney walking into a room full of 30 people, mostly strangers to each other, who had all signed up for an acting class. When I came in they were all hanging about close to the wall, with a few stilted conversations and a definite nervous tension in the air.

'Yes, and ...' was the first thing we did together and within five minutes the room was amok with fiery, mobile conversations and the noise was phenomenal.

The key here was in the two magic words, 'Yes, and ...' as opposed to 'No', 'But', and 'Maybe'. Adults have become habituated to the latter three, regarding them as a safer place to operate from, but the desire for safety stifles the free flow of thought.

I often use this one in individual voice sessions when I want people to explore their intuitive, impulsive, right-brain self.

At the same time, it's a response to that frequent request for 'more confidence'. I also use it when people come with a need to improve their capacity to think on their feet.

I love you … I hate you

Before beginning this next exercise, I would often ask the people in the room to say what is the opposite of love. Usually the response would be 'hate'.

This is an understandable misconception, but they are, once again, two sides of the same coin. The opposite of love is fear, sometimes masquerading as indifference. (A cynic is a broken-hearted romantic.) Love expands and moves towards, fear contracts and pulls away. This exercise uses a more pedestrian voice than the above extreme examples.

Exercise: 'I love you … I hate you!'

- The people in the room are paired into dyads and given a scenario, e.g. setting up camp together in the bush. All objects are mimed.
- On its own, this would likely be the set-up for some very clunky improvising, but in this instance, each person is asked to choose an attitude to operate from, either 'I love you' or 'I hate you.' (They will probably never use those actual words, this is just the subtext.)

- Now the improvisation has improved somewhat, but it is probably still a bit clunky as people settle into fixed positions. What really gives it a boost is the fact that whenever the coach taps one of the participants on the shoulder, that person changes their stance from 'I love you' to 'I hate you', or vice versa.

The need to shift instantly from one emotion to the other, takes people out of their self-conscious attachment to appearing a certain way. Otherwise to a spectator they look like people having a normal, but loaded, conversation. The key is that the flip-flopping gets people to give themselves permission to boldly inhabit the emotion.

I often say in sessions, 'I'm selling permission here. You do the rest.'

IN BRIEF

- Remove the consonants from your speech and just use the vowels which convey the emotion in the word.
- Shouting without strain requires an open throat, a slow build up, and an engaging of the whole body.
- The exercise 'Yes and' will help the ideas flow.

EPILOGUE

We all think we want to be seen and heard – indeed the notion of being ignored is painful – and yet, often when it's time to speak up and declare our self, some form of shame holds us back.

After a few decades of studying literature and theatre, I noticed that most authors are encoded with the same one, two, at most three stories that they repeat in variations. (One of the things that makes Shakespeare so special is that he has so many stories, that it's hard to track down which one is him. As Germaine Greer put it, 'there's an absence of ego'.)

I have a theory that whether or not we are artists, we each have our story that we bring to the world. If I'm right, then that means we each have a responsibility to get clear about what messages we are putting out there, to test our story to see if it rings true, to see if it adds value, to check that we're not telling ourselves a version that ultimately leads to pain and bitterness.

Charisma is sometimes defined as being comfortable in your own skin. Certainly a lot of dis-ease can come from resisting who you truly are. As Henry David Thoreau once said, 'The mass of men lead lives of quiet desperation.' (Of course, back then he didn't notice he was being gender specific, but you get the picture.)

EPILOGUE

My father used to quote this saying from time to time, and in my teens, with a whole life ahead of me, I wanted to prove him wrong. In the decades since then, I've had the luxury, which became a necessity, of looking for my authentic self.

Acting training was a great start, and when combined with personal development, meditation, therapy and voicework, the burden started to lift. The niggling questions started to fade, and it became clear that there were many authentic selves, depending on the context. The challenge became to catch the moment, to speak out and inhabit each one fully as the situation arose.

We teach what we need to know.

RESOURCES

Suggested texts for voicework

LOVE'S LABOUR'S LOST – **Shakespeare** Act 4 (iii) **Biron**
And when Love speaks, the voice of all the gods
Makes heaven drowsy with the harmony.

VERBO – Pablo Neruda
I'm going to crumple this word
I'm going to twist it,
Yes, it's too smooth
It's as if a big dog
Or a great river
Had licked it for years and years.

(If you can speak Spanish, it sounds so much better:)

Voy a arrugar esta palabra
Voy a torcerla,
Sí
Es demasiado lisa
Es como si un gran perro
O un gran río
Le hubiera repasado lengua o agua
Durante muchos años.

RICHARD III – **Shakespeare** Act 1 (ii) **Lady Anne**
Blush! Blush! Thou lump of foul deformity …
Never hung poison on a fouler toad
Out of my sight! Thou dost infect mine eyes.

GET DRUNK – Baudelaire
It is time to get drunk! If you are not to be the martyred slaves of time, be perpetually drunk! With wine with poetry with virtue, as you please, but get drunk!

REFERENCES

Page 48 'If you're interested in going a little deeper on this topic, there's an excellent ten-minute YouTube clip by Bernice McCarthy describing what she calls the 4MAT Model ...' Go to: https://www.youtube.com/watch?v=cpqQ5wUXph4

Page 82 'Research from the Harvard Business School ... shows that knowing how to take up a powerful pose helps you shift your mood and your status upwards.' For more information go to Amy Cuddy, Power Poses: https://www.youtube.com/watch?v=phcDQ0H_LnY

Page 87 'Elaine Patron, CEO and author ...' Elaine is the author *Talking Brief*, which was part of the content written for a workshop I ran.

Page 131 'A term coined in 1978 by clinical psychologists Dr Pauline Clance and Suzanne Imes, it refers to the inability of some high-achieving individuals to internalise their accomplishments and their persistent fear of being exposed as a fraud.' Dr Clance now calls it 'The Impostor Phenomenon', because it's so commonplace. Dr Pauline Clance: *The Impostor Phenomenon*. Peachtree Publishers (1985) Atlanta GA, p.

Page 138 'For those who need help getting a handle on that, the January 2017 edition of *National Geographic*, "Gender Revolution", devotes an excellent issue to a worldwide study of this topic.' *National Geographic*: Jan 2017 'The Gender Revolution'.

Page 139 'Or, to look at it another way, women now hold a paltry 4.2 per cent of CEO positions in America's 500 biggest companies.' For more information go to 2016 Fortune 500 companies with female CEOs, http://fortune.com/2016/06/06/women-ceos-fortune-500-2016/

Page 139 'There are only nine female Australian CEO's in ASX 200 companies (less than men named John).' ABC News, http://www.abc.net.au/news/2017-03-08/fewer-women-ceos-than-men-named-john/8327938

Page 140 'Firms that had women in top positions performed better.' Go to: https://www0.gsb.columbia.edu/mygsb/faculty/research/pubfiles/3063/female_representation.pdf

Page 144 'Australia has recently woken up to the disturbing statistics on domestic violence ...' For more go to Domestic Violence prevention Centre (Gold Coast,) http://www.domesticviolence.com.au/pages/domestic-violence-statistics.php

Page 150 *'Do more of what scares you most.'* 'Advice from a woman of the world' by Anneli Blundell was first published in Women's Agenda on November 2015. http://womensagenda.com.au/nab-womens-agenda-leadership-awards-2015

Page 176 'In 2013, Swedish musicologist Dr Björn Vickhoff conducted a study into the effect of music on our physiology and emotions.' For more go to: http://journal.frontiersin.org/article/10.3389/fpsyg.2013.00334/full

Page 178 'There is an excellent documentary, *The Musical Instinct: Science and Song* ...' The Musical Instinct: Science and Song https://www.youtube.com/watch?v=m5pwSMDTD4M

Page 179 'And here's one I really like: apparently black holes vibrate at B flat, a staggering 57 octaves below the waveband available to the human ear.' Go to: https://www.youtube.com/watch?v=re4WQgOxCuA

Page 191 'For a demonstration of this, search YouTube for the Osho Nadhabrahma Meditation, and for an excellent explanation of the need for active meditations, search Osho: the need for dynamic meditation. Go to: https://www.youtube.com/watch?v=pBXL6Iw-B_k&t=122s

Page 202 'We often think of the brain as being the control room, sending messages out to the body, but in fact, the belly and the heart are constantly sending messages to the brain, via the vagus nerve.' For an explanation of polyvagal theory and it's effect on voice, see Dr Stephen Porges. https://www.youtube.com/watch?v=MYXa_BX2cE8

Page 203 'There is an excellent online tutorial by Peter Levine PhD entitled Sexual Trauma: Healing the Sacred Wound.' Go to: https://www.youtube.com/watch?v=YKxHLP3HIVg

Page 206 'In her award-winning documentry...' See Putaparri and the Rainmakers.com.

Page 216 'We facilitated his growing into the role of Mike from Steven Berkoff's *East.*' *East* is a 1975 verse play by Steven Berkoff, dealing with growing up and rites of passage in London's rough East End. See *Steven Berkoff: Plays 1* (vol 1), Faber & Faber (2000), London.

ACKNOWLEDGEMENTS

Thank you to all those who helped me write this book.

First Mary, who told me I needed to do it.

To Katia for your editing know-how.

To Samantha for picking my book out of the pile and for your patience in dealing with all the to and fro it takes to print a book.

To Stefan, who was the first to read any of it.

To Gayelene for your suggestions.

And to everyone else who encouraged me along the way ... you know who you are ...